Contemporary Highlights: Risk Navigation in Financial Criminology

Muhammed Veysel Kaya / Fazlida Mohd Razali /
Yusarina Mat Isa (eds.)

Contemporary Highlights: Risk
Navigation in Financial Criminology

PETER LANG

Berlin - Bruxelles - Chennai - Lausanne - New York - Oxford

Library of Congress Cataloging-in-Publication
A record in the CIP catalog has been requested for this book
of the Library of Congress.

Bibliographic information published by the Deutsche Nationalbibliothek
The Deutsche Nationalbibliothek lists this publication in the Deutsche
Nationalbibliografie; detailed bibliographic data is available on the
Internet at http://dnb.d-nb.de.

ISBN 978-3-631-91474-8 (Print)
E-ISBN 978-3-631-91949-1 (E-PDF)
E-ISBN 978-3-631-91950-7 (E-PUB)
DOI.10.3726/b21870

© 2024 Peter Lang Group AG, Lausanne
Published by Peter Lang GmbH, Berlin, Germany

info@peterlang.com - www.peterlang.com

Contents

List of Contributors

Zaini Ahmad
Faculty of Accountancy, Universiti Teknologi MARA Cawangan Selangor, Kampus Puncak Alam, Malaysia

Ghafarullahuddin Din
Academy of Contemporary Islamic Studies, Universiti Teknologi MARA, Selangor, Malaysia

Erlane K. Ghani
Faculty of Accountancy, Universiti Teknologi MARA Cawangan Selangor, Kampus Puncak Alam, Malaysia

Aziatul Waznah Ghazali
Faculty of Economics and Management, Universiti Kebangsaan Malaysia, Malaysia

Aizad Haroon
Faculty of Accountancy, Universiti Teknologi MARA Cawangan Selangor, Kampus Puncak Alam, Malaysia

Azleen Ilias
Uniten Business School, Universiti Tenaga Nasional, Malaysia

Ainul Huda Jamil
Graduate School of Business, Universiti Kebangsaan Malaysia, Malaysia

Nur Syuhada Jasni
Faculty of Accountancy, Universiti Teknologi MARA Cawangan Selangor, Kampus Puncak Alam, Malaysia

Razana Juhaida Johari
Faculty of Accountancy, Universiti Teknologi MARA Cawangan Selangor, Kampus Puncak Alam, Malaysia

Nawal Kasim
Faculty of Accountancy, Universiti Teknologi MARA Cawangan Selangor, Kampus Puncak Alam, Malaysia

Nurliyana Khalid
School of Accounting & Finance, Taylor's University, Malaysia

Yusarina Mat Isa
Faculty of Accountancy, Universiti Teknologi MARA Cawangan Selangor, Kampus Puncak Alam, Malaysia

Maslinawati Mohamad
Accounting Research Institute, Universiti Teknologi MARA, Malaysia

Nur Arini Mohamad Rusop
Faculty of Accountancy, Universiti Teknologi MARA Cawangan Selangor, Kampus Puncak Alam, Malaysia

Nor Farizal Mohammed
Faculty of Accountancy, Universiti Teknologi MARA Cawangan Selangor, Kampus Puncak Alam, Malaysia

Fazlida Mohd Razali
Accounting Research Institute, Universiti Teknologi MARA, Malaysia

Zuraidah Mohd Sanusi
Accounting Research Institute, Universiti Teknologi MARA, Malaysia

Kamaruzzaman Muhammad
Faculty of Accountancy, Universiti Teknologi MARA Cawangan Selangor, Kampus Puncak Alam, Malaysia

Nazifah Mustaffha
Kolej Universiti Islam Antarabangsa Selangor, Malaysia

Hairul Suhaimi Nahar
Accounting Department, Faculty of Business Administration, University of Tabuk, Kingdom of Saudi Arabia

Muhammad Nazmul Hoque
Faculty of Accountancy, Universiti Teknologi MARA Cawangan Selangor, Kampus Puncak Alam, Malaysia

Normah Omar
Accounting Research Institute, Universiti Teknologi MARA, Malaysia

Vidiyanna Rizal Putri
Department of Accounting, STIE Indonesia Banking School Jakarta, Indonesia

Jamaliah Said
Accounting Research Institute, Universiti Teknologi MARA, Malaysia

Nur Aima Shafie
Accounting Research Institute, Universiti Teknologi MARA, Malaysia

Nor Aqilah Sutainim
Accounting Research Institute, Universiti Teknologi MARA, Malaysia

Sharifah Nazatul Faiza Syed Mustapha Nazri
Faculty of Accountancy, Universiti Teknologi MARA Cawangan Selangor, Kampus Puncak Alam, Malaysia

Sharifah Norzehan Syed Yusuf
Faculty of Accountancy, Universiti Teknologi MARA Cawangan Selangor, Kampus Puncak Alam, Malaysia

Roszana Tapsir
Faculty of Accountancy, Universiti Teknologi MARA Cawangan Selangor, Kampus Puncak Alam, Malaysia

Najihah Marha Yaacob
Faculty of Accountancy, Universiti Teknologi MARA Cawangan Terengganu, Kampus Dungun, Terengganu Malaysia

Nurhidayah Yahya
Accounting Research Institute, Universiti Teknologi MARA, Malaysia

Haslinda Yusoff
Faculty of Accountancy, Universiti Teknologi MARA Cawangan Selangor, Kampus Puncak Alam, Malaysia

Nor Balkish Zakaria
Accounting Research Institutes, Universiti Teknologi MARA, Malaysia

Salwa Zolkaflil
Accounting Research Institutes, Universiti Teknologi MARA, Malaysia

Lists of Figures and Graphs

Erlane K Ghani, Azleen Ilias, Kamaruzzaman Muhammad
Risk Management in Procurement in the Public Sector: A Research Opportunity

Lists of Tables

Muhammed Veysel Kaya / Fazlida Mohd Razali /
Yusarina Mat Isa

Foreword

This book is part of the series of "Global Contemporary Studies on Economics
& Business". This volume includes thirteen (13) empirical and theoretical original papers written by researchers from different countries and universities. The
target audience of this book is researchers, students and academics interested in
business, economics and social sciences.

Ahmad and Yusuf explore the fact that risk is common for business and public
life. Risk management involves identification, assessment and prioritisation of
risks. It also covers coordination and economical application of resources to
minimise, monitor and control the probability and impact of unfortunate events.
Mustaffha, Yusuf, Kassim, Tapsir, and Din identify that risks can come from uncertainty in financial markets and project failures. All industries are responsible
to conduct effective risk management that could mitigate risk occurrences in
their business operations. Another article by *Mustaffha, Yusuf, Kassim, Tapsir,
and Din* extends their research to examine the implementation of risk management in helping institutions improve the use of resources effectively and efficiently and provide better services to the stakeholders. *Khalid and Mohd Sanusi*
emphasise that every professional, regardless of their profession, needs to have
the ability to assess risk in accordance with their area or expertise, including tax
auditors and tax investigators. *Razali, Said, and Johari* reveal that high-profile
corporate scandal resulted from internal auditor failures has brought the issues
of internal auditor's risk judgment quality to the forefront and highly scrutini-
sed. Internal auditor is expected to make holistic judgment on high-risk areas
and provide an assurance on the effectiveness of company's internal control to
mitigate the risk. *Mat Isa, Mohd Sanusi, and Hoque* present the discussion in
theorising money laundering risk assessment from a behavioural perspective,
suggesting for a hybrid model which is developed based on three different theoretical foundations – i.e. behavioural decision theory, Bonner's judgment and
decision-making framework and modified Simon's model for money laundering
risk assessment. *Jamil, Mohd Sanusi, Mat Isa, and Yaacob* highlight that money
laundering is a vital attempt for criminals to evade prosecution and disguise the
unlawful origin of the illegal money from their criminal activities and fighting
money laundering is critical among financial institutions since it is significant

to protect the global economy. *Zolkaflil, Nazri, Omar, Shafie, and Ghazali* cover that borderless trading activities and the surge in internationalisation of organised crime have combined to provide the source, opportunity, and means for converting illegal proceeds into legitimate funds through money laundering operations. *Jasni and Yusoff* explore ESG challenges, particularly the intricacies of managing environmental, social, and economic aspects, focusing on supply-chain management which shows how companies must overcome internal constraints, funding limitations, and the absence of robust support systems to achieve this integration. *Haroon, Mohamad, Nahar, and Yahya* examine the pervasive issue of occupational fraud within financial institutions, elucidating the driving factors and the significant impact they pose. Occupational fraud, perpetrated mainly by employees against their employers, has emerged as a critical contributor to significant banking crises. *Putri, Zakaria, and Said* explore the financial and governmental factors influencing tax avoidance in Indonesian financial institutions, including the highlights on the self-assessment tax collection system in Indonesia, which allows taxpayers to manipulate income data and tax owed, leading to tax avoidance. *Ghani, Ilias, and Muhammad* present a comprehensive discussion of risk management, highlight a potential avenue for study pertaining to procurement within the public sector, and address the challenges often encountered in the public sector and the significance of risk management in the process of risk mitigation. *Rusop, Mohammed, and Sutainim* explore various factors influencing students' ethical perceptions, including their exam performance, family background, religiosity, and gender. Examining these factors is essential as they can shape students' ethical stances, affecting their future professional behaviour.

Zaini bt Ahmad & Sharifah Norzehan Syed Yusuf

Risk Identification

1. Introduction

Risk is common in business and public life. A dynamic market results in an organisation finding ways to reinvent its business model to self-sustain. It also increases the uncertainty of the environment where businesses and public organisations work. Business leaders face numerous challenges to ensure business remains robust and exists in the eyes of consumers. Companies have considered the importance of risk management. Risk management involves the identification, assessment and prioritisation of risks. It also covers coordination and economical application of resources to minimise, monitor and control the probability and impact of unfortunate events.

Risk identification is the first stage of risk management. Business dictionary defined risk identification as:

> Determining what risks or hazards exist or are anticipated, their characteristics, remoteness in time, duration period and possible outcome.

This means the business must identify potential risks that can jeopardise achieving the company's strategic objectives. Early and continuous risk identification is essential to prepare companies for unforeseen circumstances and reduce unwanted surprises. In other words, failure to identify potential risks will affect the company's ability to achieve performance. Indeed, risk identification should consider answering the following fundamental questions "What adverse effects in the organisation that prevent it from achieving its' goals?" The expectation is to see what could go wrong in everything and everywhere. Although it sounds unreasonable, risk identification should be continuously performed.

The objectives of risk identification are to recognise and categorise risks that could affect the business and document these risks to serve as a guide in the future. Once risks are identified, they should be classified as similar risks. This process helps reduce redundancy and ease management in later phases, that is, risk analysis. Since risk identification is the initial step of risk management, thus, the success of risk management depends on the quality of the outcome of risk identification.

2. Risk Identification Responsibilities

Usually, an organisation will assign specific staff, for example, a risk manager or risk officer, to identify potential risks an organisation faces. A risk manager's job requires a thorough understanding of a situation to enable him to recognise possible risks. If he fails to identify risks of possible losses or gains within the organisation, those risks become unmanageable. The organisation will not account for it, and the outcome could be unexpected. Thus, a risk manager is an essential function in an organisation. This is because his perception of risk will determine the future and assist in continuity planning and survival of the organisation. Specifically, risk managers' responsibilities are as follows:

1. *Advice the organisation on any potential risk* – as mentioned in the earlier section, risk managers are responsible for studying organisational risk and advising their organisations on any potential risks that may hurt, for example, the profitability or sustainability of the organisation.
2. *Put plans in place if things go wrong and decide how to avoid them* – Initial risk management plans will never be perfect. Practice, experience, and actual loss results will necessitate changes in the plan and contribute information to allow possible different decisions to be made in dealing with the risk.
3. *Provide risk analysis results and update management plans periodically.* There are two primary reasons for this:
    i. To evaluate whether the existing security controls are still applicable and practical.
    ii. To evaluate the possible changes in risk level of the business environment, for example, information risks are a good example of rapidly changing business risk.

It is not possible to discuss the specific tasks of a risk manager. Specific tasks will depend on the industries that they are working in and how specialised their role are, and will also depend on the level at which they are working. In addition to the above, the job scope of a risk manager involves the following:

- Planning, designing and implementing an overall risk management process for the organisation;
- Risk assessment, which involves analysing risks as well as identifying, describing and estimating the risks affecting the business;
- Risk evaluation, which involves comparing estimated risks with criteria established by the organisation, such as costs, legal requirements and environmental factors, and evaluating the organisation's previous handling of risks;

- Risk reporting in an appropriate way for different audiences, for example, to the board of directors so they understand the most significant risks, to business heads to ensure they are aware of risks relevant to their parts of the business and to individuals to understand their accountability for individual risks;
- Corporate governance involving external risk reporting to stakeholders;
- Carrying out processes such as purchasing insurance, implementing health and safety measures and making business continuity plans to limit risks and prepare for if things go wrong;
- Conducting audits of policy and compliance to standards, including liaison with internal and external auditors; and
- Provide support, education and training to staff to build risk awareness within the organisation.

Overall, risk managers are responsible for managing the risk of the organisation, its employees, customers, reputation, assets and the interest of stakeholders. They may work in a variety of sectors. They may specialise in several areas, including enterprise risk, corporate governance, regulatory and operational risk, business continuity, information and security risk, technology risk, and market and credit risk.

For example, look at the risk manager's role in the healthcare industry. By nature, risk managers in healthcare industries are flexible professionals and integral to delivering safe and trusted healthcare. Specifically, their role includes seeking risk in the financing, events, incident management, clinical aspects, financial aspects, legal aspects, general business aspects, healthcare's psychological and human factors, statistical analysis, insurance, and claims management.

3. Risk Identification Process

The process of risk identification can be explained as depicted in the following diagram:

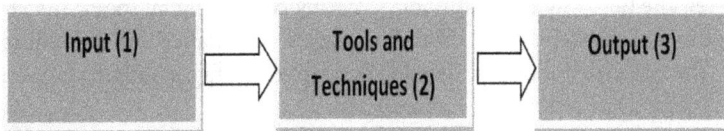

Figure 1. Risk Identification Process

3.1. Input

This stage involved identifying possible causes of business risks, the range and possible effects. A good identification of risks will be obtained by gathering detailed knowledge of the company, the industry, legal, political, social and cultural environment. Normally, a risk manager will begin risk identification by recognising key objectives of success and threads to achieve these objectives. He needs to seek for pertinent information by referring to sources of risks, such as internal and external factors. For example, business environmental factors can be obtained from published information such as commercial databases, academic studies and benchmarking.

In addition, organisational process assets represent historical information from prior project results, such as final project reports or risk response plans. Besides, the availability of lessons learned that describe problems and resolutions would help in understanding threads and corresponding actions. It is also necessary to know the scope of the project to ease the identification of risk within the scope. This information will generally be provided in the project scope statement. The risk management plan will provide information on the assignment of roles and responsibilities, budget and schedule for risk management activities and categories of risks.

Understanding the project's mission, scope and objectives of the owner, sponsor or stakeholders is crucial in risk identification. Thus, this information can also be obtained from the project management plan by reviewing the project planning documents to identify possible risks. Documents such as project charter, project scope, project schedule, cost estimate, resource plan, procurement plan, assumptions list and constraints list are helpful for properly identifying risk.

3.2. Tools and Techniques

There are several methods or tools to identify risks. The methods commonly used are document reviews, questionnaires, checklists and procedure guides. However, the best way of identifying risk is by combining all tools. The chosen method may vary depending on the industry's compliance and procedures, as well as the cultures. Below is a detailed description of five standard risk identification methods usually used to identify risk.

3.2.1. Document Reviews

Document reviews or analysis of documents is one way that would help risk managers identify risk. Usually, the process involves a structured review of the project plan and assumptions. Document review assists risk managers in identifying risks associated with the project objectives. Documents that can be reviewed are analysis of financial statements, organisation charts, the existing policies, contracts and leases, flow charts, and loss reports. Other documents that might be useful in identifying risk are minutes of Board Directors Meetings, company's manual, and annual report.

3.2.2. Information Gathering

Information gathering is also one of the most popular methods that helps identify risk. There are several ways to gather information.

i. Brainstorming

Brainstorming is the most frequently used risk identification technique. The goal is to compile a comprehensive list of risks that can be addressed later in the risk analysis process. Brainstorming involves getting subject matter experts, team members, the risk management team and anyone else who might benefit from the process in a room and asking them to start identifying possible risk events. Brainstorming begins with a meeting attended by experts in different areas. The process involves the identification of sources of risk in a broader scope, which then is categorised into their types. Brainstorming can be more effective if participants prepare in advance, the facilitator develops some risks, and the meeting is structured by project segment and risk category.

ii. Delphi Technique

Delphi's technique is more or less like brainstorming. However, the difference is that the participants do not know each other. They usually communicate using emails. The Delphi technique helps reduce bias and minimises the influence of any one person on the outcome. The process of the Delphi technique begins with the questionnaire used by the facilitator to solicit ideas about the risk. Then the facilitator will collect and compile the responses. These risks are then circulated to the experts for further comment. The consensus on the main project risks may be reached after a few rounds. This technique has been used by Shi et al. (2020) in identifying risk factors contributing to adverse events in residential aged-care facilities.

iii. Interviewing

An interview is conducted in a question-and-answer session. The appropriate people will be selected to help identify risks using their experiences, the project information and other helpful information (CIMA, 2017). Examples of people who can be interviewees are operation managers, chief financial officers, safety managers, employees, supervisors and external parties.

iv. SWOT Analysis

Strengths, weaknesses, opportunities, and threats (SWOT) is an analysis technique that examines the project's objectives, management processes, resources, organisation, and others. It also helps broaden the perspective of where to look for risks (CAANZ, 2023). Moreover, it ensures that examining the project from each SWOT perspective increases the breadth of the risks considered.

v. Checklist

The checklist is also one of the popular tools used to identify risk. The checklist is usually developed using historical information and experience from past projects. A checklist should be considered incomplete, and the possibility of other risks should also be addressed. Two familiar checklists can be used.

Exposure Checklist

An exposure checklist is a listing of common exposures. Usually, it is used to jot the memory before and after inspections. This technique, however, is not suggested to be used during inspection.

Insurance Policy Checklist

Insurance policy checklist is a list that normally includes a catalogue of the various policies or types of insurance that a given business might need. For example, one of the most useful and widely used is Coverage Applicable, published by the Rough Notes Company.

Assumption Analysis

Assumption analysis is a technique that explores the assumption's accuracy. It identifies risks to the project and minimises inaccuracy, inconsistency, or incomplete assumptions.

Diagramming Techniques

This technique assists by providing a diagram showing the cause and effect – for example, system or process flowcharts. Causes of risks would be identified easily, as the diagram will show how various system elements interrelate and the causation mechanism.

Questionnaires

A questionnaire is focused on detecting the concerns of staff to risks or threads that they perceive in their operating environment. It is also called a fact-finder because it helps managers in detecting risk through a series of detailed and penetrating questions. Sometimes, questionnaires are designed to include both insurable and uninsurable risks.

3.3. Output

The output for risk identification is the "list of identified risks with description". This list will be included in the risk register, a record documenting the results of risk identification processes.

4. Classification of Risk

Risks must be classified or categorised concerning their origin to be more structured. Classification of risks can be done with sector, financial, competitors, suppliers, customers, operational and technology as follows:

Sector

Risks under this category are external and can significantly influence the achievement of an organisation's objectives and strategies – for example, regulatory changes, business fragmentation, the appearance of new markets, etc.

Financial

Financial risks are uncertainty associated with the availability of financing, the exchange rate, volatility of interest rate, and insufficient knowledge on sources/methods of financing.

Competitors

It is associated with the risks of a businessman. A businessman needs to consider the existence of new competitors, how intense the competition is and whether it is a specialised competition or not.

Suppliers

Suppliers' risks include variation in terms of the price of raw materials, variety in the supply, the availability of supply, quality of supply, as well as methods of payment.

Customers

Customers' risks can stem from changes in customers' tastes and needs, urging for reduction in price pressuring for quality of products and requesting lengthy payment methods.

Operational

These are risks associated with successfully implementing strategies into specific plans through effective allocation of resources. Operational risks involved, the need for advertisement, the cost of recruiting staff, the possibility of centralisation or decentralisation, the need for good operational and financial planning, etc.

Technology

Risks related to technology. These risks are derived from the need to undertake significant investment (e.g. heavy machines) to ensure business projects are completed within the stipulated time or train employees to use those machines.

5. Challenges in Risk Identification

There are always challenges that we have to face in whatever we do. In the risk identification process, various challenges can impact the organisation. Challenges in the risk identification process will be significant if an organisation needs to establish proper decision-making mechanisms and adequate and functional internal controls. A functional procedure appropriately solves internal problems (Hilton, 2023). An adequate policy directs employees on how to perform tasks and report problems. Those challenges are:

1. Assessing risk in a context of uncertainty
2. Complexity of the risk
3. Lack of availability of investigated information
4. Personnel are reluctant to cooperate with the risk management team
5. Process in dealing with various perceptions
6. Time constraints

Assessing risk in uncertainty becomes the biggest challenge for risk managers. Uncertainty is said to be the heart of risks. It reflects the need for more knowledge about future events' impact and occurrence. Uncertainty involves when there is more than one possible outcome and where the future conditions are unknown. There will always be some difference between the estimated and the actual costs and benefits that are eventually realised. These differences can arise because of inherent biases in developing the cost-benefit analysis or because of risks or uncertainties not foreseen when the analysis was undertaken.

A student says, "I am certain I will get an A in this course", which means the same as "I am positive I will get an A in this course". Both statements reflect a conviction about the outcome. Uncertainty, on the other hand, is the opposite mental state. If one says, "I am uncertain what grade I am going to get in this course", the statement reflects a lack of knowledge about the outcome. Uncertainty is simply a psychological reaction to the absence of knowledge about the future. The existence of risk is a condition or combination of circumstances in which there is a possibility of loss that creates uncertainty on the part of individuals when the risk is recognised.

The complexity of the risk is another challenge. In assessing the risk, there are a few complex processes that the risk manager must take up. It requires a combination of scientific and technical knowledge, not just from the experts in business activities but also from those who understand the consequences of decisions for business and the economy. Complexity is the degree to which a system or component has a design or implementation that needs to be understood and verified. Whereby, inherently, complexity is the degree of complication of a system or system component, determined by such factors as the number and complexity of interfaces, the number of complexities of conditional branches, the degree of nesting, and the types of data structure. For example, the complexity of the risk can happen because of the organisation's activity itself which is very complicated.

According to Vilko and Hallikas (2012), complexity and disintegration become major challenges in supply-chain risk management. Supply chains in the modern world are complicated networks that stretch over longer and longer distances, which makes them vulnerable to a variety of risks. Global supply chains require highly coordinated goods, services, information, and money flows within and across national boundaries. The value of holistic views is required to face those risks in the risk identification and risk assessment process. In the healthcare industry, the growing complexity process requires management approaches considering multiple points of view.

With respect to the study made by Jian et al. (2011), there needs to be more investigation information in this risk identification process. The limited information can create some errors in the probability estimated. The lack of information needed can lead to the poor quality of results and a partially completed risk identification process. Therefore, the risk management team will still need to achieve their objectives in managing those risks.

In the risk identification process, the primary input comes from the organisation's personnel, a specialist with extensive experience. The risk management faces difficulties in completing this process if the *personnel are reluctant to cooperate with the risk management team*. To identify those risks, the risk management team must fully understand the process involved in an organisation's activity. The team will require personnel with the most experience in the organisation's activities to guide them. This is because different industries will have different types of risk. The risk management team will not have enough knowledge in those industries to enable them to decide. They need support from the organisation's personnel, and finding those willing to cooperate with the team is usually tough. They are reluctant to cooperate, especially when the risk management team is an outsider hired by the top management to manage the organisation's risks.

The *process of dealing with various perceptions of* risks can also be a challenge in risk identification. There is an idea that actual risks often diverge dramatically from their perception. What is implied by the fact that different people, societies, and nations seem to have very different perceptions of the same risk? Usually, the perception of risk is different from one another. This can cause different people to find different ways of analysing the risk. According to Tingley, Asmundsson et al. (2010), risk is a subjective concept that can be perceived differently by different groups and is a composite of subjective influences, values and expectations of future events.

Finally, the time constraint will be one of the challenges that the risk management team will have to face. Hlaing et al. (2008) stated that, in the construction activities, the *time constraints* will be the significant challenges in the risk identification process. This is because construction production is mainly employed just in time for the client's production requirement. So, the risk manager will not have enough time to analyse the risks that might occur from the projects. The time constraint implies that the risk manager might be unable to identify more risks and find the best way to mitigate those risks. Therefore, the possibility of the risk to occur is very high.

In conclusion, the future is unpredictable. To successfully identify risk and meet the objectives, the risk management team should be able to overcome those challenges first by having expertise in that particular area and managing time wisely. That expertise might be able to handle the complexity of the risk and understand more about the organisation's activities. There are methods available that can be used to help the organisation in identifying and assessing the risks. So, the management can choose the most appropriate method to identify the organisation's risks to meet the objectives.

Finally, a suitable risk identification must match the assessment type required to support risk-informed decision-making. This means the risk manager must first understand the multiple types of risk assessments, such as programme risk assessments to support an investment decision, analysis of alternatives, and assessments of operational or cost uncertainty to enable him to come out with quality risk identification.

Acknowledgement

The authors would like to extend their gratitude to the Accounting Research Institute, HiCOE and Universiti Teknologi MARA for funding this research under the Bestari Grant – Islamic Financial Criminology, with reference number 600-RMC/DANA 5/3/BESTARI (TD) (010/2022)

References

Association of Chartered Certified Accountants (ACCA). (2019). *Strategic business leadership*. BPP Learning Media UK.

Association of Chartered Certified Accountants (ACCA). (2019). *Advanced performance management*. BPP Learning Media UK.

Chartered Accountants Australia and New Zealand. (2023). *Business performance*. John Wiley & Sons.

Chartered Accountants Australia and New Zealand (CAANZ). (2023). *Risks and technology*. John Wiley & Sons.

Chartered Institute of Management Accountants (CIMA). (2017). *Strategic management*. BPP Learning Media UK.

Chartered Institute of Management Accountants (CIMA). (2017). *Risk management*. BPP Learning Media UK.

Hillson, D. (2023). *The risk management handbook: A practical guide to managing the multiple dimensions of risk* (416 pp.). Kogan Page Publishers. 9781398610651. https://books.google.com.my/books?id=xevMEAAAQBAJ.

Hlaing, N. N., Singh, D., Tiong, R. L. K., & Ehrlich, M. (2008). Perceptions of Singapore construction contractors on construction risk identification. *Journal of Financial Management of Property and Construction*, *13*(2), 85–95. https://doi.org/10.1108/13664380810898104

Jian, H. U., Chu, J., Liu, J., & Dayong, Q. (2011). Risk identification of sudden water pollution on fuzzy fault tree in Beibu-Gulf Economic Zone. *Procedia Environmental Sciences, 10,* 2413–2419. 10.1016/j.proenv.2011.09.375

Shi, C., Zhang, Y., Li, C., Li, P., & Zhu, H. (2020). Using the Delphi method to identify risk factors contributing to adverse events in residential aged care facilities. *Risk Management and Healthcare Policy, 13,* 523–537.

Tingley, D., Ásmundsson, J., Borodzicz, E., Conides, A., Drakeford, B., Edvardsson, I., Holm, D., Kapiris, K., Kuikka, S., & Mortensen, B. (2010). Risk identification and perception in the fisheries sector: Comparisons between the Faroes, Greece, Iceland and UK. *Marine Policy, 34,* 1249–1260. 10.1016/j.marpol.2010.05.002

Vilko, J. P. P., & Hallikas, J. M. (2012). Risk assessment in multimodal supply chains. *International Journal of Production Economics, 140*(2), 586–595.

Nazifah Mustaffha, Sharifah Norzehan Syed Yusuf, Nawal
Kasim, Roszana Tapsir, & Ghafarullahuddin Din

Risk Transfer and Risk Retention in the Banking, Construction, Extractive, and Insurance Industries

1. Overview on Risk Transfer and Risk Retention

Risk transfer is considered one of the main strategies for protecting corporate assets and shareholder values. On the other hand, risk retention is defined as a viable strategy for small risks where the cost of insuring against risk would be greater over time than the total losses incurred. All risks that are not avoided or transferred are retained by default. Once risks are identified, an organisation must continuously manage them by ways of retention or transferring the risks. In today's business growth, all assessed risks are monitored and managed. The organisation's decision to ignore the risk, and retain or transfer the risk is one critical element that determines the corporate value (Dionne, 2013). This decision determines the potential effects and extent of disruption to corporate assets, customers, reputation, and shareholder value. Inappropriate decisions in transferring risk may harm the organisation's system and consequently affect the whole transaction and procedures.

2. Risk Transfer and Risk Retention by Specific Industries

The execution of risk transfer and retention in business practices draws different pictures from different business industries. This section elaborates on two risk management concepts, namely risk transfer and risk retention in four different industries. The four industries are banking, construction, extractive, and insurance. This section provides guidelines on the management of potential risks through effective strategies and solutions by each industry.

2.1. Banking Industry

The banking institutions endure potential financial risks due to the rapid challenges of the financial market. In line with the development of technological innovation, the banks are looking forward to improving and implementing greater systems that can always fulfil customer needs. However, despite the main challenges, the banks need to balance between profit optimisation and risk management through financial risk transfer and risk retention. An unsecured banking system is known to be exposed to more risk potentials and thus could result in the losing end to the banking institutions. Therefore, banks should find strategic solutions for implementing effective risk transfer or securing risk retention that can increase the value of services and products. In order to construct an effective control system, the banks should establish an integrated risk management that incorporates risk awareness into the bank's procedures, policies, or routine activities. Apart from that, strong enforcement of risk management should be emphasised among the bank personnel and management so that better results can be produced.

Most banks are exposed to risks such as credit risk, operational risk, liquidity risk, and market risk. Credit risk is commonly associated with the potential loss resulting from the default of the counterparty in fulfilling its obligations at the designated time. There are three components related to credit risk, namely, credit exposure, probability of default, and loss default. Operational risk involves with errors and fraud occurring in banking transactions such as payment errors or settling transactions and is also related to human behaviour. Liquidity risk is caused by a stressful and unfavourable cash flow over a short period. If a firm has highly liquid assets and is suddenly in need of cash, then it will liquidate some of its assets at a discount. Finally, market risk correlates with changes in the price of financial assets and liabilities (market conditions) and impact on the investment portfolio (Adamowicz, 2018). Each financial risk highlights the different trends in the banking and financial industry, thus determining the appropriate risk transfers and retention. The following explains further about each risk in the respective industry.

2.1.1. Credit Risk

Credit risk relates to the potential loss due to default from the customer's credit records. The customer is referred to the respective party that is individually or corporately involved directly or indirectly with the banking activities. The customers are the heart of the banking and financial institutions as they are the sources of income. Fulfilling customer's rights is the main priority of the banks. Somehow, the banks should not simply aim for high numbers of customers but should also be concerned with other important elements such as good credit background checking, effective credit portfolio analysis as well as efficient collection/payment strategies which could help the banks to mitigate credit risk threats. A research study conducted by Tafri et al. (2011) supported the need to measure credit risk in a standardised manner which is supported by external credit assessments while the other alternative is to use internal rating. Thus, good internal policies and effective external measurement could form an effective credit risk retention strategy in banking credit activities.

In order to implement credit risk management, the banks will revise and come out with new guidelines on transferring potential credit risks (Bank Negara Malaysia, 2023). Normally, the Unit of Credit Risk Management will be assigned to assess the customer's credit rating based on the assessment of relevant factors which include the customer's financial position, types of facilities, and securities offered before the credits are approved by the relevant approving parties. The review is conducted once a year with updated information on the customer's financial position, market position, industry, and economic condition.

2.1.2. Market Risk

Market risk is risk of losses in earnings and capital resulting from changes in market prices and interest rates. The risks appear when the banking transactions were exposed to customers' driven activity and proprietary trading. The main categories of the market risks that the banking institutions need to quantify are:

(a) Interest rate risk which arises from changes in yield curves, credit spreads and implied volatilities on interest rate options.
(b) Foreign exchange rate risk which arises from changes in exchange rates and implied volatilities on foreign exchange options.
(c) Commodity price risk which arises from changes in commodity prices and commodity option implied volatilities.
(d) Equity price risk which arises from changes in the price of equities, equity indices, equity baskets, and implied volatilities on related options.

The above risks provide significant impacts for the banking institutions to implement effective risk management by taking into account the targeted volumes, market volatility, business sales, and niche of products and services. The identified risk management should be able to control the interest changes, facilitate high returns, and reduce volatility in price changes in commodities, highlighting transparent market risk and liquidity risk profile. The different approaches between Islamic banks and conventional banks in managing potential risks have shown contrary results. Siddiqui (2008) argued that Malaysian banks engaging in Islamic financing have lower credit and liquidity risks, but higher interest rate risks compared to conventional banks.

2.1.3. Liquidity Risk

The liquidity risk in the banking institution is well defined as the prospective and current risk to earn and raise the capital means from a bank's inability to fulfil its obligations when due without incurring any unacceptable losses. In other words, liquidity risk involves the inability to fund increases in assets, managing the unplanned changes in fund sourcing, and meeting the obligations when required, without incurring additional costs or encouraging a cash flow crisis. Primarily, effective and efficient liquidity risk management policies and frameworks will ensure that a bank has enough excess liquid assets to cover the liabilities that fall due in the short term and to manage any unexpected demands for funds by its depositors or creditors (Basel Committee on Banking Supervision, 2008). Thus, the implementation of an effective bank's liquidity risk management determines the level of position that the bank may suffer cash flow crisis and unexpected costs excess.

According to Van der Vossen (2010), the holding of liquid assets in excess of requirements is considered a liquidity cushion or buffer which helps the bank in times of increased liquidity pressure to meet liquidity needs. The tremendous financial market demands have alerted the banking institution to increase the liquidity ratio at the same time transfer the existing and potential liquidity risks through effective portfolio system. The leading framework and practices by the national bank of the country can help the banking institution to form stronger foundation in managing and measuring its liquidity risk exposures.

Furthermore, the initiatives taken such as controlling liquidity gap, indicate early warning signals, perform liquidity indicators, and conduct stress testing will derive better results. The establishment of policies and procedure in the internal system itself will help to increase liquidity positions of the banks in terms of monitoring basis. Through close monitoring, the diversification of the liquidity structure in assets and liability position will meet the fund requirements that derived from interbank deposit transfer, customer deposits, swap market, bank loan, debt securities, medium term funds and also loan syndication. Most banking institutions have also initiated and conducted the backup strategy to cover the fund requirements such as bank's standby lines with external parties on the need basis. The sources of liquidity are regularly reviewed to maintain a wide diversification hence to secure the short and long terms expectations.

2.1.4. Operational Risk

Generally, the operational risk is defined as the risk of loss resulting from inefficient and failure of internal system, process and people or occurrence from external events. Operating risks in the banking transactions occur within the operation circle internally and externally. As it involves inter-relations with management and bank personnel, vendors and as well as the customer, the operating risk differs with other bank risks as it is not meant to generate profit but to focus more on human behaviour, system entity and processing involved in daily banking transactions. However, other risks need to be concerned particularly on operating risks because improving the systems or correcting the errors for the benefit that they will receive on cost involved determining the appetite for operating risk. In managing operational risk, the banks should be able to estimate the probabilities of events occurring and financial loss derived for each banking activity.

For example, the use of internet banking facilities among customers would expose to operational risk which refers to customer identification hacking, invalid transactions, or illegal fund transfers. Therefore, the bank should implement tight security of the internet banking system to transfer operational risks in order to gain higher customer confidence in online banking security. Jaruwachirathanakul and Fink (2005) supported the argument that the perception of good security is the presence of a third party on the website guaranteeing security and the appearance of a privacy statement that promises the minimisation of risk and privacy breaches to potential internet banking users.

After all, the role of the operational risk management committee in banking institutions is important to ensure the execution and implementation of the operational risk management framework, tools and policies are in place as well as the continuity of business planning in operation events. The committees also take charge of executing operational risk mitigation strategies and controls for the operation activities. This includes conducting risk awareness programmes for their staff on operational risk management policies, frameworks, policies, governance, and tools. Thus, the strong combination of internal and external operational risk management through effective risk transfer strategies can provide better overall outcomes.

2.2. Construction Industry

Basically, construction is a process that consists of building or assembling infrastructure. Construction projects have many unique features, such as long periods, complicated processes, abominable environments, financial intensity, and dynamic organisation structures. Such organisational and technological complexity generates a lot of risks and severity. In addition, the diverse interests of stakeholders in a construction project further provide risks. Since some of the risks cannot be eliminated, it is essential for the construction company to effectively identify and manage risks wisely.

Risk is perceived as the potential for unwanted or negative consequences of an event or activity. It comprises a combination of hazards and exposure that may have harmful effects on the construction project. In order to mitigate and manage risk, construction companies need to implement risk assessments for every project that they have or currently constructing. Risk management is a system that aims to identify and quantify all risks to which the business or project is exposed. Risk management is related to the process of risk management planning, identification, analysis, implementation and responses, and monitoring and control of a project.

The risk management process begins with risk identification. In other words, it involves identifying any potential risk associated with a construction project. In the integrative part of risk identification, risk classification attempts to structure the diverse risks affecting a construction project. Once the risks of a project have been identified and analysed, the appropriate risk implementation or response strategies must be adopted to cope with the risks in the project implementation. The treatment to measure risk is based on the nature and impact of the risk. The main aim of risk management is to remove as much as possible the potential negative impact and to increase the level of control of the risks. However, in real practice, the risk management process is to identify appropriate strategies to assist project stakeholders in managing risks.

Lyons and Skitmore (2004) concluded that risk reduction is the most frequently used risk response method, followed by risk transfer, risk elimination, and risk retention in the Queensland engineering construction industry. Akintoye and MacLeod (1997) found that most contractors transfer risks to their specialist sub-contractors through insurance premiums. A review of previous studies found that the construction industry prefers to transfer risk through specialists and financial transfer. Insurance and exclusion clauses in contracts are the most popular way of transferring risks financially. Risk reduction is the most frequently utilised risk response method. On the other hand, Baker et al found risk reduction is the most frequently utilised risk response method. Over 90% of the respondents in their research suggested the constant use of risk reduction techniques. Risk transfer is next with risk retention being used the least.

Managing risks in construction projects is a very important process in achieving project objectives in terms of time, cost, quality, safety, and environmental sustainability. To tackle these risks appropriately, construction companies must seek the best strategies to manage risks wisely. The management plays an important role in managing risks through sustaining sufficient training and education as well as communication between two parties. Abdul-Tharim et al. (2011) found that the best ways to mitigate risk in construction industries are through communication and management control. Zou et al. (2007) extended the findings on the key risks in construction projects in China, such as project funding problems, contractors' poor management ability, difficulty in reimbursement, unwillingness to buy insurance, and lack of awareness of construction safety and pollution.

In the construction industry, there is a big probability that workers can be exposed to injury risks. Larsson and Field (2002) examined injury risks in the Victorian construction industry and found fall risks are the absolute priority for injury prevention among the major occupational groups in the Victorian construction industry.

In his study, several risks related to occupational were identified such as:

 i. Painters – Falls from height, especially ladders and stepladders
 ii. Crane, Earthmoving Operators – Falls and manual handling of vehicle attachments
iii. Bricklayers – Falls from height, predominantly from scaffolding
 iv. Plasterers – Falls from equipment they stand on while working
  v. Tilers, pavers, concreters – Manual materials handling
 vi. Steelworkers – Falls from height, falling objects, power tools
vii. Roof layers – Falls from roof, power tools
viii. Plumbers – Falls from height
 ix. Carpenters – Power tools and falls from height
  x. Electricians – Falls from height, electrical safety
 xi. Other construction workers – Falls from height, power tools

According to Lyon and Skitmore (2004), there is no single risk assessment technique that fits all cases that could mitigate risks. There is no absolute method for dealing with risks, be it risk avoidance, reduction, retention, transfer, or sharing. In other words, the selection of risk assessment method depends on the nature of the risks.

2.3. Extractive Industry

The extractive industry refers to activities involving the extraction of natural sources from the earth to be used by consumers. These include any activities that remove minerals, metals, and aggregate from the earth. For example, oil and gas extraction and mining and quarrying. The nature of this industry imposes future uncertainty events due to operational risk, safety and environmental pressure, and government regulation. Begg et al. (2002) explained that this industry deals with a higher risk that could affect everyone; therefore, it is evident that proper risk management needs to be developed to manage uncertainty in the future. It is acknowledged that risk cannot be eliminated but must be managed. Aven et al. (2007) mentioned that there is a need to have risk management in an organisation to develop a proper framework in obtaining the proper balance to exploring new opportunities by mitigating accident and natural disaster. Decision from risk management in the situation of uncertainty and dealing with high risk and the decision to be made will be a consequence to the industry. Various problems have to be faced by the industry that need attention.

One of the risks faced by this industry is naturally occurring radioactive material (NORM). According to Cowie et al. (2012), NORM can be referred to as hazards that happen in pipelines, waste products of oil production, machinery, and plants that cause potential radiological health hazards. Employees who use equipment that is contaminated by NORM may be exposed to the radiation. On the other hand, waste material from the industry should be properly maintained to avoid contamination to the public. However, if the waste material indicates positive of NORM, the industry will be facing problems in ensuring the general public, workforce and the environment is being protected from the associated hazards.

Cowie (2012) did research on one of the Oil and Gas Companies in Saudi Arabia. The Company had employed several ways to solve the contamination of NORM. The five key elements being used to manage contamination are NORM monitoring, safe management of NORM – NORM-contaminated equipment, control of NORM waste, workers protection and training, and sharing the best practices. The process involves managing the NORM in the early stages, preventing contamination, and implementing the required support from all staff in the company.

The first stage is NORM monitoring. At this stage, a survey was conducted on employees who may be exposed to contamination for protection guidelines. Then, an inspection in the facilities where NORM is suspected was done. If the existence of NORM is detected, proper procedure is implemented to protect the employees in order to minimise contamination in the workplace. The next stage is the management of NORM-contaminated equipment. This stage was conducted with the objective to create and implement procedure in identifying equipment that may be exposed to NORM. This was done by using radiation detection device. The equipment exposed to contamination was isolated and stored in a designated area. The equipment was then decontaminated for future use. The third stage involved NORM management with the main aim of temporary storage solutions. The objective of this stage is to prevent uncontrolled and improper disposal of NORM waste through the provision of quick, effective, and easy-to-implement solutions to the operating facility. This includes controlling NORM waste on a temporary basis before implementing permanent disposal of NORM waste.

Another stage is employees' protection. At this stage, the management creates awareness among the employees on NORM contamination by providing training for protection measures and contamination control to workers who deal directly with NORM contamination. The final stage involved sharing experiences by interacting with other oil companies that work in the field of NORM management. In addition, pipelines need to be considered as an effective way of transporting especially in the oil and gas industry. The pipeline needs to be well maintained to avoid the possibility of a pipeline leak that may cause a natural disaster. Today offshore pipelines are more effective than before, and leak of chemical is minimal.

However, Dey et al. (2004) found that if such a problem occurs, it can have a bad impact on both the environment and habitat. The use of pipelines is considered the safest way to transport oil and gas rather than using the highway in which failure may occur due to natural disasters and human error. Dey et al. (2004) in their findings found that the failure may be due to several factors such as external influence, internal and external corrosion, material defect, operation error, and other natural hazards. He found that internal corrosion is the main factor of pipeline failure and suggested the effective way to solve this problem is by replacing it with a new one. Other than that, frequent maintenance using diving and sampling is performed to avoid future failure.

Based on another study conducted in China, the researcher adopted dynamic operational risk assessment (DORA) as a technique in the oil and gas industry. This methodology assesses the probability of the operational mode failure of a system. Yang and Mannan (2010) found that, since the stochastic modelling considers system abnormal events in addition to component failure, the DORA methodology aids in incident prevention as it examines the system's degraded behaviour due to component abnormal events before a failure actually occurs. The dynamic analysis provides the possibility of preventing system dysfunction. The implementation of DORA needs continuous monitoring and updating of safety programme components such as risk-based and cost-effective monitoring.

A study by Bigliani (2011) has shown that nowadays extractive industry faces risk volatility in commodity prices which is not influenced by supply and demand but more affected by socio-economic factors such as safety workforce, environmental protection, and government regulations. The study also provides the possibilities of risks that may occur such as cyber threats, cost overrun, and risk of non-compliance, and the problems can be mitigated by using information technology. In the extractive industry, project portfolio is complex and risky, and managing it often requires large capital. The industry needs to make strategic decisions about which project shall be prioritised first to ensure that the company would act in the best performance, especially in processes that involve drilling and exploration of new resources. Failure to organise it will expose the company to higher risk and substantial losses. As a result, the project needs to be properly evaluated in the list of projects should be constantly revised, new projects are evaluated and prioritised based on the level of risk associated together with expected return to the business.

Bigliani (2011) provided four actions that can be used to mitigate operational risk in the oil and gas industry. First, the industry needs to organise the right information at the right time. The industry needs to continue developing intelligence forms of technical and business data. The data collected would be used to conduct drilling and exploration of new resources with the ultimate goal of reducing risk and meeting compliance requirements with information life-cycle management.

The second action is the prevention of non-compliance. The industry needs to face regulatory pressure from the government because different countries may have their own regulation. The problems become more complicated when a company has few subsidiaries that operate in different countries. The company needs to follow local regulations to ensure the project proposal is approved including approval for drilling to minimise risk and ensure regulatory compliance. In addition, investment in environmental, health, and safety (EHS) should be prioritised since the government will first look at company safety procedures before approval to operate in the country is granted. Every company must develop its own EHS procedure. The EHS is a set of applications and technologies that facilitate the necessary flow of compliance actions such as inspection and reporting.

Another action that can be taken is a "holistic approach to operational and enterprise risks". Information technology plays an important role in mitigating operational risk and enterprise risk management. The industry needs tactical and strategic plan decisions about their asset, whether they are resources, reserves, or facilities. In order to reduce the possibility of operational risk, the industry can use information technology such as using governance, risk, and compliance (GRC) software. This software will sort the document and verify the business control which includes audit management, corporate policy, financial compliance, and continuous enterprise controls monitoring.

The last action is "cyber-security policy design and execution". In order to compete in the complex and sophisticated business environment, every company needs expertise and higher security of business information systems. Due to the complexity of this industry, expertise is needed to help smoothen business operations. For example, with the complexity of drilling and operation, industries need high-end 3-D visualisation and collaboration rooms that allow global teams to access the same data, models, and tools.

2.4. Insurance Industry

The insurance industry today faces a unique set of long-term and short-term challenges. Underwriting risks are impacted by well-known long-term trends such as greater longevity and an increasingly unpredictable climate. Principal among these challenges is the current turmoil in the financial markets which is impacting the insurance industry in multiple ways, such as eroding value in the investment portfolio, increasing default risk, and making it harder to raise capital. The insurance industry has evolved from a one-dimensional technical policy provider to a diversified entity that is now able to understand further the potential risks that cause injury to organisations.

Insurance is a financial topic of paramount importance for every individual. It is designed to protect the financial well-being of an individual and his dependents in the case of unexpected loss. Some forms of insurance are required by law, while others are optional. Agreeing to the terms of an insurance policy creates a contract between an individual and the insurance company. In exchange for payments from the individual known as premiums, the insurance company agrees to pay the individual a sum of money upon the occurrence of a specific event. That event may be as mundane as a visit to the doctor or as serious as a car crash, depending on the type of insurance.

Although various types of insurance were introduced, the truth is, there are only two main types of insurance that cover different aspects of our life, namely general insurance and life insurance. Life insurance is an insurance coverage that pays out a certain amount to the insured or their specified beneficiaries upon a certain event such as the death of the individual who is insured. The risks that are covered by life insurance are premature death, income during retirement, and illness. Basically, general insurance is an insurance policy that protects individuals against losses and damages other than those covered by life insurance. For more comprehensive coverage, it is vital to know about the risks covered to ensure those individuals are protected from unforeseen losses.

The risks that are covered by general insurance are property loss such as a burnt house or stolen car, liability arising from damage caused by yourself to a third party, and accidental death or injury. Insurance is one of the best risk transfer methods that should be used by other industries to avoid or minimise the risk occurring in their firm. However, like other sectors, insurance may also face certain risks such as premium risk, investment risk, reinsurance contribution risks, recovery risks, claim risks, interest and dividend risks, reinsurance cession risks, adviser risks, tax risks, and cross-disciplines risks.

2.4.1. Insurance and Risks

In the insurance sector, awareness and commitment to risk management at all levels within the organisation are critical for the effective implementation of risk management plans. This may be achieved in many ways such as:

   i. Obtaining commitment and active ongoing support from senior managers for implementation of risk management policy and plan.
  ii. Appointing a senior manager (or team) to actively lead and sponsor risk management initiatives.
 iii. Establishing a team responsible for communicating the risk management policy and plan.
  iv. Incorporating risk management awareness sessions into existing staff forums such as Toolbox Talks', staff meetings, workshops, and training sessions.
   v. Incorporation of responsibilities and performance measures for managing risk in job descriptions of all staff.

The successful implementation of effective risk management programmes throughout the organisation largely depends on the support of senior management. A change in management plan may be needed to ensure the coordination of activities across the organisation and the involvement of staff from operational areas. One key consequence of risk in the insurance sector is financial distress. Clandre (2006) noted that distress is important to insurance companies since insurance pricing normally becomes more economically attractive during times of distress. For example, the price of directors' and officer's insurance hardened dramatically following the post "new economy" accounting misconduct of Worldcom, Enron, etc.

Therefore, for an insurance company to be well positioned during distress times, it must ensure that it does not let itself fall prey to distress. There are a variety of techniques to manage distress at the enterprise level. For example, insurance-operational distress could be managed through corporate-driven reengineering initiatives which perhaps could have helped rectify the suboptimal growth-related policies and practices. Similarly, financial distress could be addressed through restructuring which would have improved reliance on capital structure and in turn, would have likely brought the firm's managers some time to reengineer their way out of the distress. Under the new technology, the insurance sector has also faced cyber risks. In this situation, the insurance industry is attempting to understand the nature of cybercrime issues and how to more accurately design insurance policies for the future. In an effort to protect against unlawful electronic or physical activity, organisations are now taking a closer look at their implementations and what is needed to protect confidential assets. The ill effects or inabilities have proven costly to the insurance industry and have triggered a sense of desire to define more efficient controls to mitigate the burden of settlement. Insurance companies are realising the need to implement greater assessment capabilities to determine the state of an organisation's security infrastructure when examining an organisation's request for coverage.

Moreover, natural disaster insurance plays a key role in the context of transfer risk. A further challenge for the insurance sector is to transfer a portion of the risk to the capital markets and to serve the better needs of the poor. The following are the three steps in managing the risk from natural disasters:

1. Identification of the hazards.
2. Evaluation of the risk, where risk is a function of hazard, exposed values, or human lives and the vulnerability of the exposed objects.
3. Controlling and financing future losses.

The mechanisms described above have been developed to cope with well-known disasters such as earthquakes, windstorms, and floods. They can be applied, in principle, also to lessen well-investigated and less frequent extreme disasters such as submarine slides, great volcanic eruptions, meteorite impacts and tsunamis which may arise from all these hazards.

An insurance perspective risk consists of three components, namely: hazard, vulnerability of objects exposed to a hazard, and value of the exposed objects. The hazard is usually defined as the exceeded probability of an event of a specified minimum size. For example, the wind velocity in the case of windstorms or the ground shaking in the case of earthquakes. The vulnerability is expressed as the expected average loss as a percentage of the replacement value and depends on the hazard. For disaster prevention, this financial definition of vulnerability should be supplemented by loss of life. Furthermore, insurance companies are exposed to various credit, market, and insurance risks in the course of their business.

Broadly, they can manage these risks in three ways:

- Arrange for another entity to take on the risk at the outset. For example, a bank might arrange a bond issue for a corporate customer rather than lending it-self, or an insurance company might arrange for a customer to "self-insure" by establishing a captive insurance company rather than buying insurance cover.
- Retain risks in their balance sheets and seek to control them through careful monitoring, pricing and diversification.
- Hold the risk only temporarily before selling it to a secondary market, hedging it with another offsetting transaction or repackaging it to sell or hedge it.

2.4.2. Insurance and Risk Management Strategies

In the insurance sector, risk management strategies fall into three broad categories:

1. *Prevention strategies – to reduce the probability of a downside risk.*

These are introduced before a risk occurs. Reducing the probability of an adverse risk increases people's expected income and reduces income variance (both increase welfare). Strategies to prevent or reduce the occurrence of income risks have a very broad range that surpasses the traditional scope of Social Protection (SP). These include policies regarding sound macroeconomics, public health, the environment, education, and training. Preventive SP interventions are typically linked to measurement in reducing risks in the labour market, notably the risk of unemployment or under-employment, or low wages due to inappropriate skills or poorly functioning labour markets. They are concerned with labour standards and the functioning of the labour market, resulting from skill mismatch, bad labour market regulations, or other distortions.

2. *Mitigation strategies – to decrease the potential impact of a future downside risk.*

As with reduction strategies, mitigation strategies are also employed before risk occurs. Whereas preventive strategies reduce the probability of the risk occurring, mitigation strategies reduce the potential impact if the risk occurs. Risk mitigation can take several forms such as:

- Portfolio diversification reduces the variability of income by relying on a variety of assets from which returns are not perfectly correlated. This requires the acquisition and management of different assets such as physical, financial, human, and social capital in their different forms. For example, if individuals can only invest in human capital, they can still diversify in different occupations but perhaps to the detriment of the return. If women cannot own or inherit land and have no access to safe financial instruments, they may acquire gold and jewels.

- Informal and formal insurance mechanisms are characterised by risk sharing (i.e. risk pooling) through several participants whose risks are not (much) correlated. While formal insurance benefits from a large pool of participants of which results in less correlated risks, informal insurance has the advantage of low information asymmetry. The characteristic of formal or market-based insurance such as the payment of a risk-based insurance premium that gives rise to future state-contingent payments is often straightforward. Informal insurance arrangements are more difficult to be described as they come in different and often disguised forms because one "institution" serves insurance and non-insurance type functions (such as the family and the community). Hedging has an increased importance for financial markets (e.g. forward exchange rate contracts) and is based on risk exchange or payment of a risk price to somebody for assuming that risk. Yet these arrangements do not appear to work in a labour income-related and formal provision environment the effects of asymmetric information are too strong. However, elements can be found in informal arrangements. For example, various family arrangements (marriage) and some labour contracts are more akin to hedging than insurance.

3. Coping strategies – to relieve the impact of the risk once it has occurred.

The main forms of coping consist of individuals or households dis-saving or borrowing, migration, enhancing labour supply (including that of children), reduction of food intake, or reliance on public or private transfers. The government plays an important role in assisting people in coping. For example, in the case where individual households have not saved enough to handle repeated or catastrophic risks. Individuals may have been poor for their entire lifetime with little or no possibility to accumulate assets, being rendered destitute by the smallest income loss and running the risk of being exposed with irreversible damages.

3. Conclusion

In conclusion, the implementation of effective risk management through risk transfer strategies and risk retention could assist an organisation in achieving better results in business operations. Regardless of the industry background, the organisation itself should initiate an efficient internal and external system that can accommodate the challenges and demands in the financial market on a competitive basis. Nevertheless, the adoption of technological innovation and the improvement of personnel and management expertise are also important to support the effectiveness of the risk management strategies.

Acknowledgement

The authors would like to extend their gratitude to the Accounting Research Institute, HiCOE and Universiti Teknologi MARA for funding this research under the Bestari Grant – Islamic Financial Criminology, with reference number 600-RMC/DANA 5/3/BESTARI (TD) (010/2022)

References

Abdul-Tharim, A. H., Jaffar, N., Lop, N. S., & Mohd-Kamar, I. F. (2011). Ergonomic risk controls in construction industry – A literature review. *Procedia Engineering*, 20, 80–88.

Adamowicz, T. (2018). Types of risk in banking operations – categorization and definitions. *Economic and Regional Studies (Studia Ekonomiczne i Regionalne)*, *11*(673–2019–911), 37–56.

Akintoye, A. S., & MacLeod, M. J. (1997). Risk analysis and management in construction. *International Journal of Project Management*, *15*(1), 31–38.

Aven, T. (2007). A unified framework for risk and vulnerability analysis covering both safety and security. *Reliability Engineering & System Safety*, *92*(6), 745–754.

Bank Negara Malaysia. (2023). *Credit risk*. Bank Negara Malaysia. https://www.bnm.gov.my/documents/20124/938039/pd_Credit_Risk_2023.pdf

Basel Committee on Banking Supervision. (2008). *Principles for sound liquidity risk management and supervision*. Bank for International Settlements.

Begg, S., Bratvold, R., & Campbell, J. (2002, September). The value of flexibility in managing uncertainty in oil and gas investments. In *SPE Annual Technical Conference and Exhibition?* (pp. SPE-77586). SPE.

Bigliani, R. (2013). Reducing risk in oil and gas operations. *IDC Energy Insights*, (May), 1–15.

Cowie, M., Mously, K., Fageeha, O., & Nassar, R. (2012). NORM management in the oil and gas industry. *Annals of the ICRP*, *41*(3–4), 318–331.

Dey, P. K., Ogunlana, S. O., & Naksuksakul, S. (2004). Risk-based maintenance model for offshore oil and gas pipelines: A case study. *Journal of Quality in Maintenance Engineering*, *10*(3), 169–183.

Dionne, G. (2013). Risk management: History, definition and critique (September 6, 2013). *Risk Management and Insurance Review, 16*(2), 147–166.

Jaruwachirathanakul, B., & Fink, D. (2005). Internet banking adoption strategies for a developing country: The case of Thailand. *Internet Research, 15*(3), 295–311.

Larsson, T. J., & Field, B. (2002). The distribution of occupational injury risks in the Victorian construction industry. *Safety Science, 40*(5), 439–456.

Lyons, T., & Skitmore, M. (2004). Project risk management in the Queensland engineering construction industry: A survey. *International Journal of Project Management, 22*(1), 51–61.

Oliva, F. L. (2016). A maturity model for enterprise risk management. *International Journal of Production Economics, 173*, 66–79.

Osman, A., & Lew, C. C. (2021). Developing a framework of institutional risk culture for strategic decision-making. *Journal of Risk Research, 24*(9), 1072–1085.

Siddiqui, A. (2008). Financial contracts, risk and performance of Islamic banking. *Managerial Finance, 34*(10), 680–694.

Tafri, F. H., Rahman, R. A., & Omar, N. (2011). Empirical evidence on the risk management tools practised in Islamic and conventional banks. *Qualitative Research in Financial Markets, 3*(2), 86–104.

Van der Vossen, B. (2010). Bank liquidity management. *Business/Business Administration, 39.* https://scholarsarchive.library.albany.edu/honorscollege_business/39

Yang, X., & Mannan, M. S. (2010). The development and application of dynamic operational risk assessment in oil/gas and chemical process industry. *Reliability Engineering & System Safety, 95*(7), 806–815.

Zou, P. X., Zhang, G., & Wang, J. (2007). Understanding the key risks in construction projects in China. *International Journal of Project Management, 25*(6), 601–614.

Nazifah Mustaffha, Sharifah Norzehan Syed Yusuf, Nawal
Kasim, Roszana Tapsir, & Ghafarullahuddin Din

Risk Management Framework for Zakat Institution

1. Introduction

A review of the literature indicates that the Enterprise Risk Management (ERM) framework is the best practice, and it can be applied in the governance of zakat institutions. Based on MS ISO 31000:2010, this study proposes a risk management framework that is tailored to suit the unique mission, risk contexts, and risk profiles of zakat institutions. Generally, this article serves as a general guideline for the zakat institutions to implement risk management effectively in achieving the noble objective of zakat.

Increased concerns regarding corporate accountability in various types of organisations have been associated with the need for appropriate risk management systems. This is due to complex challenges and various risks faced by the organisations currently due to global exposure and complex operations. These phenomena require an organisation to have effective management and governance to achieve the organisation's goals and objectives. Zakat institutions are not excluded from facing such challenges. They are exposed to the same phenomena, consistent with their expansion towards corporatisation and growth in their operations in terms of collection and disbursement functions.

Zakat institutions are trusted bodies responsible for managing zakat funds. Zakat institution plays a vital role in providing the highest level of development for *asnaf* life, as well as ensuring the sustainability of the Muslim economic system. Besides fulfilling a Shariah requirement, it has been identified as one of the public institutions that need to be managed, organised, and administered effectively and efficiently. With the emergence of advanced technologies worldwide, managing zakat funds become more challenging due to environmental and socio-economic shifts in modern societies. As a result, some of the zakat institutions themselves have moved towards corporatisation by adopting certain corporate strategies that best suit the nature of zakat institutions.

The recent performance of the zakat institutions, particularly in Malaysia, reflects the complexity and challenges in managing the public and religious funds to achieve the noble objectives of zakat in Islam. This indicates higher risk exposures faced by zakat institutions. Thus, it is very crucial for institutions to have proper and effective risk management procedures to achieve better performance in the future and convince the public of their ability to manage zakat funds effectively and efficiently. Thus, this chapter outlines a general framework as a guideline for zakat institutions to practice risk management in their institutions based on the literature review and risk management framework of MS ISO 31000:2010.

2. Zakat Management

Zakat management and administration in Malaysia falls under the jurisdiction of states, i.e. under the State Islamic Religious Council (SIRC) except in the Federal Territories where it is governed by the Federal Government (Salleh, 2014; Wahab & Abdul Rahman, 2011). The law of zakat in the states is provided under their Islamic Enactments respectively. Since the Enactments differ from one state to another, the rules governing the zakat matters, including the organisational structure, zakatable items as well as the punishment for various zakat-related offences are different among the states (Bakar et al., 2014; Zainal et al., 2016). Zakat Institutions are bodies in Muslim societies, of which the functions are similar to an Inland Revenue department on the one hand and a social welfare organisation on the other. The core activities of zakat institutions are collecting compulsory payments from eligible Muslims and distributing them to the rightful beneficiaries. These organisations provide various kinds of assistance such as food, shelter, health, and education to rightful beneficiaries. In the literature (DiMaggio & Powell, 1983), such a social welfare organisation is known as a human service organisation. The uniqueness of a zakat institution as compared to other social welfare organisations is that it has to abide by Islamic principles as outlined by the Shariah comprising of the Holy Quran, Sunnah, and Islamic Jurisprudence. The main idea of establishing a zakat institution is to ensure that all funds collected from eligible Muslims can be distributed to rightful beneficiaries. Zakat institutions in Malaysia are categorised into four management models (Makhtar et al., 2016).

The first model refers to zakat collection and distribution functions under the distinctive zakat institution governance, which is separated from the state's Islamic Religious Enactment. This model is applied by Lembaga Zakat Negeri Kedah (LZNK) and Tabung Baitulmal Sarawak. Both institutions are established under Enakmen Lembaga Zakat Negeri Kedah Darul Aman 2015 and Ordinance of Sarawak Islamic Council (Incorporation) (Revised) 1984, respectively, which is different enactment from the SIRC's enactment. The second model reflects the fully corporatised zakat institutions, in which zakat collection and distribution functions are managed by a single corporatised zakat institution established under the Administration of State Islamic Religious Enactment of the respective SIRC. This model was adopted by Lembaga Zakat Selangor (LZS) and Penang Zakat Centre which were established under the Trustees (Incorporation) Act 1952 (Revised 1981) and Company Act 1965, respectively.

The third management model refers to the semi-corporatised zakat institutions, where the zakat collection and distribution function are segregated between corporatised zakat institutions under the Administration of State Islamic Religious Enactment of the respective SIRC and Baitulmal or Zakat Division of SIRCs. This model is adopted by the Federal Territory, Malacca, Negeri Sembilan, and Pahang. Finally, the fourth model refers to the non-corporatised zakat institutions that manage both zakat collection and distribution functions directly under the respective SIRCs. This model is applied by the SIRCs of Johor, Perlis, Perak, Kelantan, Terengganu, and Sabah.

Historically, zakat management and administration in Malaysia has evolved from a traditional way to a modern technique when Majlis Agama Islam Wilayah Persekutuan (MAIWP) Kuala Lumpur or Kuala Lumpur Federal Territory Islamic Council (FTIC) initiated adoption of corporate management technique into their zakat collection management. This is called the process of corporatisation of the zakat institutions, where zakat management transformation begins in this country. The idea of corporatisation is aimed to improve the efficiency and effectiveness of the zakat collection system in Kuala Lumpur. Previous studies have shown that the corporatisation of several zakat institutions has improved the zakat management of the institutions. Specifically, before 1990, all zakat-related matters in zakat institutions such as information with regard to zakat payers and recipients as well as collection and disbursement of zakat were managed manually. Post-corporatisation in the 1990s, technology such as computerised systems have been used especially by the corporatised zakat institutions to replace manual zakat management gradually (Pusat Pungutan Zakat Wilayah Persekutuan, 2017). As a result, fully corporatised zakat institutions perform better than semi-corporatised zakat institutions in terms of zakat collection, which was assessed based on their zakat performance index (Mohd Noor et al., 2015; Nahar, 2018). This performance at least signals that there is an increase in the public's confidence towards zakat management by the zakat institutions in Malaysia.

3. Issues in Zakat Management

Islam provides strict guidelines from the Holy Quran and Sunnah for those employed to administer zakat funds. The Shariah emphasises that zakat administrators must safeguard the zakat funds collected and ensure that the zakat fund is
spent appropriately and goes to the rightful beneficiaries of zakat (Al-Qardhawi,
1999; Farishta, 2003). Syed Musa (2005) supported the importance of proper
zakat collection and distribution. He asserted that zakat institutions need to be
effective and efficient in administering zakat funds to ensure that the objectives
of zakat can be achieved. Farishta (2003) emphasised that it is necessary to ensure zakat institutions are free from mismanagement and corruption. Hence,
zakat administrators must ensure that the implementation of zakat is within the
guidelines stipulated by the Shariah.

For present-day zakat institutions to be freed from negligence and embezzlement of zakat funds, the zakat management must conform to Shariah, the rules
and regulations as stipulated in the Holy Quran and the Sunnah. No matter how
long the lapse of time between the Prophet Muhammad's (PBUH) management
and the present, the basic principles for governing zakat institutions remain (Al-
Qardhawi, 1999; Farishta, 2003; Nik Mustapha, 1991; Rosli & Mohd Fikri, 2007;
Syed Musa, 2005). This is expressed in the Holy Quran:

> We said: Get ye down all from here; and if, as is sure, there comes to you guidance
> from me, whosoever follows My guidance on them shall be no fear, nor shall they
> grieve. (2:38)

Today, the chances of misappropriation or mismanagement of zakat funds are
greater compared to those days. More Muslims now deviate from the teachings
of Islam (Ahmad Jais, 2010). In order to avoid negligence, Farishta (2003) suggests that contemporary zakat management must include both collection and
distribution functions in an organised manner. Al-Qardhawi (1999) explained
that the collection function should include collecting, keeping records, gathering
information and safeguarding the zakat funds. He added that the duty of zakat
administrators should also be to identify zakat payers. Zakat administrators must
keep databases for all zakat payers. Al-Qardhawi (2009) further emphasised that
zakat administrators must be proactive. This is consistent with Mujaini (2005)
who believes that zakat administrators must take initiatives to improve and be
able to plan to ensure whatever amount zakat payers have paid is sufficient to
purify their wealth. If the zakat administrators perform these activities well, the
chances of negligence may be minimised or totally avoided.

Monitoring zakat collection, distribution and safeguarding the funds from misappropriation are important elements in zakat management. Farishta (2003) outlined financial control elements such as having proper receipts to keep track of zakat payments. She also emphasised that disciplinary action must be taken against officials who misappropriate zakat funds. As stated by Al-Qardhawi (1999), the Prophet Muhammad (PBUH) Himself was strict in safeguarding public funds and took matters like misappropriation and fraudulent acts in administering zakat very seriously. In the Sunnah Adi ibn Umayra reports the Prophet Muhammad said:

> Whoever is employed in any collection jobs and hides from us even a needle or more, it is misappropriation, and he will bear what he misappropriated on the Day of Judgement.

In another Sunnah, as reported by Muslim, a Black man from Ansar said to Prophet Muhammad (PBUH):

> "O Messenger of Allah, accept my resignation from the job." The Prophet Muhammad asked, "Why?" and the man replied, "I heard you saying (such and such)". The Prophet (PBUH) continued, "And I say now, whoever we employ in a job must bring forward what he collects, the little and the big. What we give him after that, he should take, and what we do not give him, he should leave alone."

Both the above Sunnah clearly indicate that negligence or misappropriation is not accepted in Islam and Muslims must avoid them in any actions, particularly in zakat management. Being an institution that collects a substantial amount of funds, zakat bodies are exposed to various risk that relates to safeguarding of the funds.

Despite the rapid transformation of the Malaysian zakat institutions, the public still gets suspicious about their governance (Johari et al., 2015; Kaslam & Bahrom, 2007; Salleh, 2014). Among the issues found include (i) a long waiting period to process the application, where the potential recipients need to wait three weeks to know the results of their application, and (ii) inefficient dissemination of information regarding the zakat sources and performance (Ahmad et al., 2015; Johari et al., 2015). Most importantly, issues of corruption among zakat managers (Muzammir, 2017) and zakat collection by unauthorised amils who collect zakat using own-printed receipts (Bernama, June 10, 2018) jeopardise the reputation of zakat institutions in the eyes of potential zakat payers.

Lastly, there is an issue with zakat awareness among the public, especially among business owners on business zakat which is still considered low. It was reported that only about 20% of Muslim business owners paid business zakat (Wahab & Rahman, 2012). This situation seems unresolved when recently it was reported that business zakat awareness in Terengganu (Bakar, 2016) and the Federal Territory is still low (Amry & Fiona, 2018). These issues expose the zakat institutions to reputation risks that will lead to collection and distribution risks. Moving forward, good rapport between the zakat institutions is very important to promote and inculcate awareness among the potential zakat payers, especially business zakat payers. Thus, zakat institutions should play crucial roles in mitigating those risks as one of the efforts to improve their governance and performance and subsequently portray good rapport to the public at large. The problems and challenges found in the previous studies reflect the exposure of zakat institutions to various types of risks that need further investigation.

4. Risk and Risk Management

Risk is referred to "*uncertainty and the results of uncertainty*" (Harrow, 1997) and "the possibility of danger, loss, injury or other adverse consequences" (Collier et al., 2006). This reflects to a lack of expectedness about a problem structure and/ or its consequences in any decision or planning situation. Meanwhile, MS ISO 31000:2010 further defines risk as "effect of uncertainty on objectives and it helps decision making process by taking account of uncertainty and its consequences on achieving objectives and assessing the need for any action" (Department of Standards Malaysia, 2010). The consequences of risks may contribute to opportunities for benefit (positive impact of risks) or threats to success (negative impact) of the organisation (Institute of Risk Management, 2002).

Risk management is defined by the Islamic Financial Services Board (2005) as "a process that consists of risk identification, measurement, mitigation, monitoring, reporting and control". This is in line with ISO 31000 definition of risk management which is "coordinated activities to direct and control an organization with regards to risks". These activities form part of the risk management framework which includes designing, implementing, monitoring, reviewing, and continually improving risk management throughout the organisations (ISO 31000: 2010). Simply, the focus of risk management are identification and treatment of potential risks that harm the performance of an organisation. Its objective is to add maximum sustainable value to all the activities of an organisation. Thus, it improves achievement, and reduces both the probability of failure and the uncertainty of achieving the organisation's overall objectives (IRM, 2002). Moreover, risk management is a continuous process that depends on changes in the internal and external environment of an organisation. These changes in the environment require continuous attention for the identification of risk and risk control (Abu Hussain & Al-Ajmi, 2012). As risks continue to grow and evolve in line with the advancement of technology, risk management capability is also improving towards becoming more complex.

Due to its importance, risk management is recognised as a key activity for all corporations, financial institutions, and other types of organisations, including zakat institutions. Risk management is a forward-looking approach in managing the possibilities of risks from occurrence which may hinder organisation to achieve its objectives. Ismail (2010) defines risk management as "the process by which managers satisfy the need to manage institution's risk exposure by identifying key risk factors; obtaining consistent, understandable, operational risk measures; choosing which risk to reduce, and which to increase and by what means; and establishing procedures to monitor the resulting risk positions". Particularly, the implementation of risk management helps institution to improve their management, use resources effectively and efficiently and provide better services to the stakeholders (Collier et al., 2006). Obviously, risk management plays an important role in reducing and eliminating the costs of risk, in making the most effective and efficient use of taxpayer's money (or zakat payers' money in the case of zakat institutions), and in protecting the well-being of communities. Since it finally affects not only the institution, failure to implement an effective risk management programme will finally jeopardise the community at large (Qiao, 2007). Accordingly, having risk management in practice is good for an institution.

5. Risk Management and Zakat Institution

Few studies had been conducted on risk management of zakat institutions (Ascarya et al., 2016; Dyarini & Jamilah, 2017; Rahmatika & Hariono, 2018). Among the top risks encountered by zakat institutions in Indonesia is strategic, education, amil and volunteer, law as well as compliance risks. The most severe risk is related to operational risk. Specifically, zakat institution faces zakat collection risk due to bad reputation and lack of education on the obligation of paying zakat among zakat payers. The institutions also expose to risk associated to zakat distribution (e.g. late distribution and zakat misallocation to non-asnaf) as well as fund management operation (e.g. incompetent and insufficient staff and inefficiency in managing zakat funds) (Ascarya et al., 2016: Dyarini, 2017).

In view of the severity of the risk in zakat collection and distribution, zakat institutions have taken the initiative to implement risk management practices. In Malaysia, several challenges are faced by the zakat institution in their efforts to implement risk management. Due to its infancy of implementation, the main challenge is a lack of understanding and awareness with regard to risk management and its importance among the zakat institution managers (Ali et al., 2019). This will lead to the low acceptance of risk management in their institution. Furthermore, zakat institutions have lack of or no internal risk management experts. Thus, few zakat institutions have sought for external experts to help them realise the effort to implement risk management (Ali et al., 2019).

Regardless of the challenges, few efforts have been initiated by several zakat institutions to implement risk management in their institutions. For example, Malaysia, as represented by Lembaga Zakat Selangor and Pusat Pungutan Zakat have involved in the efforts to develop (i) International Standard of Zakat Management (ISZM) 2017 (World Zakat Forum, 2017) and (ii) Zakat Core Principles (ZCP) (Beik et al., 2014). These two working committees are based in Indonesia. Both the ISZM 2017 and ZCP cover the standard requirements and guidelines covering the aspect of risk management. Observing the extensive efforts initiated by several zakat institutions in practising risk management, there is a crucial need to establish a risk management framework as general guidelines for zakat institutions to implement risk management effectively.

6. Proposed Risk Management Framework for Zakat Institutions

Risk management is a crucial element that needs to be implemented efficiently by any organisation including zakat institutions to achieve their mission and vision. Since zakat institutions manage significant financial resources, thus risk management is important to improve their performance and subsequently enable zakat institutions to be a catalyst in improving the lives of the poor and needy (Mahyuddin & Abdullah, 2011).

Figure 1 illustrates the proposed component of risk management framework for the institution, based on the MS ISO 31000:2010. The standard is used as the basis for the adaption of the framework because the standard is based on the ISO 31000, which is the latest, internationally recognised, industry-neutral and most intuitive standard. It contains a clear process description and harmonised language (Abu Bakar, 2014) making it a good base for zakat institutions' specific framework.

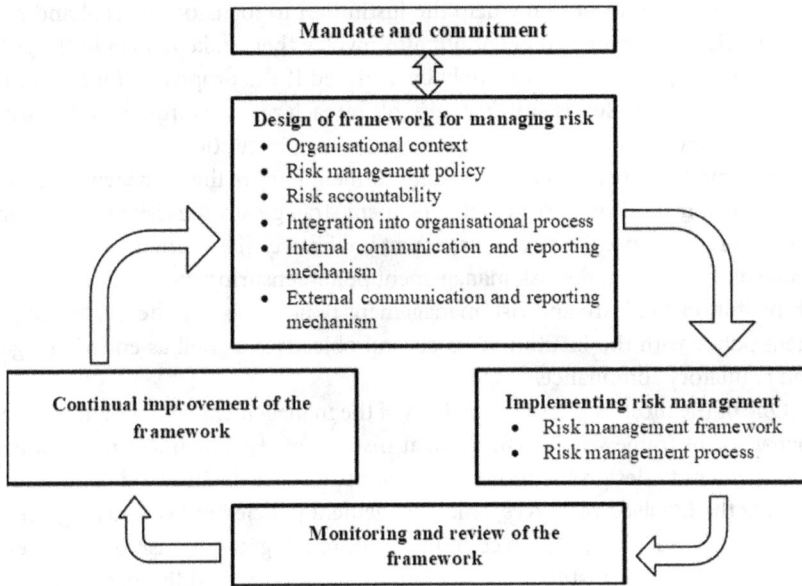

```
┌─────────────────────────────────────────┐
│         Mandate and commitment          │
└─────────────────────────────────────────┘
                    ⇕
┌─────────────────────────────────────────┐
│ Design of framework for managing risk   │
│  • Organisational context               │
│  • Risk management policy               │
│  • Risk accountability                  │
│  • Integration into organisational      │
│    process                              │
│  • Internal communication and reporting │
│    mechanism                            │
│  • External communication and reporting │
│    mechanism                            │
└─────────────────────────────────────────┘
┌──────────────────────┐  ┌───────────────────────────────┐
│ Continual improvement│  │ Implementing risk management  │
│ of the framework     │  │  • Risk management framework   │
│                      │  │  • Risk management process     │
└──────────────────────┘  └───────────────────────────────┘
        ┌─────────────────────────────────────┐
        │   Monitoring and review of the      │
        │           framework                 │
        └─────────────────────────────────────┘
```

Figure 1. Proposed Components of Risk Management Framework (Based on MS ISO 31000)

Basically, the framework is not intended to prescribe a management system, but rather to assist the institution to integrate risk management into its overall management system. Therefore, institutions should adapt the components of the framework in accordance with their specific needs. If an institution's existing management practices and processes include components of risk management or if the institution has already adopted a formal risk management process for particular types of risk or situations, then these should be critically reviewed and assessed against the Risk Management Standard in order to determine their adequacy and effectiveness (MS ISO 31000). The major goal for the adaptation of MS ISO 31000 is to assist zakat institutions to minimise risks in their daily operation and management. This framework covers holistically operational areas and key strategic management areas. The framework covers internal and external elements of the institution to effectively capture potential risks that may arise in these areas.

Hence, this proposed framework intends to assist zakat institutions in implementing risk management practices specifically in identifying, assessing, and managing the existing and potential risks without focusing on one specific area.

Additionally, it does not only help the institution to focus on internal and external risks in their environment but also involve their stakeholders in the risk management process. This can only be achieved if the proposed framework is easily understandable, yet still customisable by each zakat institution and adjustable to the nature, needs, and requirements of each institution.

First and foremost, mandate and commitment require the management team of the zakat institution to plan and implement strategically the risk management framework to ensure the risk management is effective. The mandate includes defining and endorsing the risk management policy, ensuring the synchronisation of institutional culture and risk management policy, aligning the risk management policy with the institution's goals and objectives as well as ensuring legal and regulatory compliance.

One of the most important mandates of the management is to design the risk management framework for their zakat institution. This mandate requires the management to design the framework that fits to their institutional context, including the involved resources, risk management policies and risk management accountabilities. Then, they need to plan how to integrate the risk management policies within the institutional operation and process. Additionally, the risk management activities need to be communicated and reported internally within the institution and externally to the public to increase and establish their accountability and transparency to the stakeholders.

As for the implementation phase, the institution should implement the developed framework effectively and efficiently. Thus, they need to define the appropriate timing and strategy to apply the risk management policy and implement the risk management process while complying with legal and regulatory requirements. The risk management process includes risk identification, risk analysis, risk evaluation and risk treatment. This process should be applied through a risk management plan at all relevant levels, departments, and functions of the institution.

The risk management framework should be monitored and reviewed periodically to ensure its effectiveness and relevancy in supporting the institutional performance. In this phase, the institution should measure risk management performance against indicators, which are periodically reviewed for appropriateness and in line with the risk management plan. In case of inefficiency, the existing risk management framework needs to be revised and amended accordingly for continual improvement of the framework.

7. Conclusion

Generally, zakat institutions in Malaysia have experienced tremendous growth in terms of collection and distribution. However, despite the growth in the collection and distribution of zakat, zakat institutions are exposed to various types of risks that may affect their performance and subsequently influence the public's confidence to pay zakat to the formal zakat institution.

Since every institution is exposed to risks, it is responsible to cater and manage the risks wisely and effectively. However, due to the absence of proper risk management guidelines, the way they manage risks might be different from one state to another. Due to this scenario, the present study proposes a basic framework of risk management for zakat institutions, that can be tailored to the nature of individual zakat institutions since every institution may differ in terms of governance practice.

Future research should be undertaken to evaluate how zakat institutions manage their risks with or without proper risk management procedures, depending on the availability of the procedures within the institution.

Acknowledgement

The authors would like to extend their gratitude to the Accounting Research Institute, HiCOE and Universiti Teknologi MARA for funding this research under the Bestari Grant – Islamic Financial Criminology, with reference number 600-RMC/DANA 5/3/BESTARI (TD) (010/2022)

References

Abu Bakar, N. A. (2014). Principles and guidelines international standards for the management of risk. In *Seminar on MS ISO 31000: 2010 Risk Management*.

Abu Hussain, H., & Al- Ajmi, J. (2012). Risk management practices of conventional and Islamic banks in Bahrain. *The Journal of Risk Finance*, *13*(3): 215–239.

Ahmad Jais, A. (2010). Memberi Makna Kepada Kehidupan. *Solusi*, *2*.

Ali, A., Mohamad Nor, M. N., Shafie, R., & Wan Ahmad, W. N. (2019). Implementation of good risk management practices for zakat institution. *International Journal of Zakat and Islamic Philanthropy*, *1*(1), 45–52.

Al-Qardhawi, Y. (1999). *Fiqh az-Zakah*. Dar Al-Taqwa.

Amry, S. O., & Fiona, J. (2018, April 10). *Zakat perniagaan, ramai kurang kesedaran*. Berita Harian Online. https://www.bharian.com.my/berita/nasional/2018/04/410281/zakat-perniagaan-ramai-kurang-kesedaran

Ascarya, R. S., & Beik, I. S. (2016). Merancang Manajemen Risiko Pengelolaan Zakat (Issue November).

Bakar, A. A. (2016, June 12). Kesedaran bayar zakat perniagaan masih rendah – MAIDAM. Berita Harian Online. https://www.bharian.com.my/taxonomy/term/2645/2016/06/163562/kesedaran-bayar-zakat-perniagaan-masih-rendah-maidam

Bakar, A. A. A., Ibrahim, M. A., & Noh, S. M. (2014). *Zakat management and taxation*. Islamic Banking & Finance Institute Malaysia (IBFIM).

Beik, I. S., Nursechafia, Muljawan, D., Yumanita, D., Fiona, A., & Nazar, J. K. (2014). *Towards an establishment of an efficient and sound zakat system*. Working paper presented in the Working Group of Zakat Core Principles 2014.

Bernama. (June 10, 2018). http://www.astroawani.com/berita-malaysia/hati-hati-kutipanzakat-fitrah-tidak-bertauliah-di-kedah-lznk-177803

Collier, P. M., Bery, A. J., & Burke, G. T. (2006). *Risk and management accounting: Best practice guidelines for enterprise-wide internal control procedures* (Research Executive Summaries Series, Vol. 2, No. 11). CIMA Publishing.

Department of Standards Malaysia. (2010). *MS ISO 31000:2010 Risk management – principle and guideline*.

DiMaggio, P. J., & Powell, W. W. (1983). The iron cage revisited: Institutional isomorphism and collective rationality in organizational fields. *American Sociological Review*, 48(2), 147–160.

Dyarini, D., & Jamilah, S. (2017). Manajemen risiko pengelolaan zakat. *Ikraith-Humaniora*, 1(2), 45–52.

Farishta, G. d. Z. (2003). *The law and institution of zakat* (2nd ed.). The Other Press.

Institute of Risk Management (IRM). (2002). *A risk management standard*.

Islamic Financial Services Board (IFSB). (2005). IFSB-1 – guiding principles of risk management for institutions (other than insurance institutions) offering only Islamic financial services.

Ismail, A. G. (2010). *Money, Islamic banks and the real economy*. Cengage Learning Asia Pte. Ltd.

Johari, F., Ali, A. F. M., & Aziz, M. R. A. (2015). A review of literatures on current zakat issues: An analysis between 2003–2013. *International Review of Research in Emerging Markets and the Global Economy*, 1(2), 336–363.

Kaslam, S., & Bahrom, H. (2007). Amalan "Corporate Governance" dalam Pengurusan Institusi Zakat di Malaysia. *Jurnal Pengurusan JAWHAR*, 1(2), 53–70.

Mahyuddin, A. B., & Abdullah, A. G. (2011). Towards achieving the quality of life in the management of zakat distribution to the rightful recipients (the poor and needy). *International Journal of Business and Social Science, 2*(4), 237–245.

Majid, M. Z. A. (2003). *Pengurusan Zakat.* Dewan Bahasa dan Pustaka.

Makhtar, A. S., Ahmad, S., Zain, M. N. M., & Nasohah, Z. (2016). *Transformasi Pengurusan Zakat dan Model Pelaksanaannya di Malaysia* (pp. 485–498). Persidangan Antarabangsa Perundangan Islam.

Mujaini, T. (2005). Zakah Dalam Dunia Mutakhir: Keperluan Kajian dan Analisis Ilmiah Kontemporari. *Isu-Isu Kontemporari Zakat di Malaysia, 1.*

Muzamir, M. Y. (2017, July 19). *CEO, pegawai Zakat Pulau Pinang didakwa rasuah.* Berita Harian Online. https://www.bharian.com.my/berita/kes/2017/07/303661/ceo-pegawai-zakat-pulau-pinang-didakwa-rasuah

Nahar, H. S. (2018). Exploring stakeholders' views on a corporatized zakat institution's management performance. *International Journal of Ethics and Systems.*

Nik Mustapha, N. H. (1991). Zakat in Malaysia: Present and future status. In N. Hassan (Ed.), *Development and finance in Islam.* IIU.

Press Pusat Pungutan Zakat Wilayah Persekutuan. (2017). *Laporan Zakat PPZ 2017.*

Qiao, Y. (2007). Public risk management: Development and financing. *Journal of Public Budgeting, Accounting & Financial Management, 19*(1), 33–55.

Rahmatika, A. N., & Hariono, T. (2018). Risk management of zakat maal supervision in the Fintech era based on literature review. *International Conference of Zakat 2018,* pp. 195–201.

Rosli, M., & Mohd Fikri, C. H. (2007). *Maqasid Al-Syariah: Hikmah di Sebalik Pensyariatan* (1st ed.). Karya Bestari Sdn Bhd.

Salleh, M. S. (2014). Organizational and definitional reconfiguration of zakat management. *International Journal of Education and Research, 2*(5), 61–70.

Syed Musa, A. (Ed.). (2005). *Zakat recognition and measurement of business wealth: An analysis of the growth Condition* (1st ed.). UPM Press.

Wahab, N. A., & Rahman, A. R. A. (2011). A framework to analyze the efficiency and governance of zakat institutions. *Journal of Islamic Accounting and Business Research, 2*(1), 43–62.

Wahab, N. A., & Rahman, A. R. A. (2012). Efficiency of zakat institutions in Malaysia: An application of data envelopment analysis. *Journal of Economic Cooperation & Development, 33*(1).

Zainal, H., Bakar, A. A., & Saad, R. A.-J. (2016). Satisfaction of zakat distribution, and service quality as determinant of stakeholder trust in zakat institutions. *International Journal of Economics and Financial Issues, 6*(S7), 72–76.

Nurliyana Haji Khalid & Zuraidah Mohd Sanusi

Tax Fraud Risk Judgment: The Lens of Tax Auditors and Tax Investigators

1. Introduction

Tax is one of the important sources of revenue, particularly for developing countries including Malaysia (Ngah et al., 2022). The money collected from taxes is used to fund a variety of government initiatives as well as better citizen services like infrastructure, defence, healthcare, and education. It serves as a means of income redistribution from the rich to the poor in addition to generating cash for the state coffers (Miskam et al., 2013). As a result, it is now a crucial tool that the government uses to carry out a variety of policies meant to enhance the welfare of the populace and the nation's development (Mohamad, Zakaria & Hamid, 2016).

Although tax collection income is crucial for the government, there is a significant prevalence of tax fraud instances particularly in the corporate sectors that need to be reduced (Kasipillai & Chen, 2014). The government's loss of revenue is substantial and more concerning as it grows gradually over the years, despite the implementation of different steps by the tax authority to ensure tax compliance (Zakaria et al., 2013). If tax fraud activities are not mitigated, they will harm society and the economy. Not only does it diminish the government's revenue, but it also has the potential to significantly impair the effective functioning of the government (Lai et al., 2013). In addition, increasing tax fraud cases diminished public confidence in the tax system and structure.

The tax authority of the Malaysian government is the Inland Revenue Board of Malaysia (IRBM), which is officially registered under the Ministry of Finance. The main role of IRBM is to offer services related to the management, evaluation, collection, and enforcement of direct taxes under the Income Tax Act (ITA) 1967, Petroleum (Income Tax) Act 1967, Real Property Gains Tax Act 1976, Promotion of Investments Act 1949, and Labuan Business Activity Tax Act 1990 (IRBM, 2022). According to the 2022 Annual Report of IRBM (IRBM, 2022), tax revenue remains the major contributor to total revenue, comprising the largest portion of the Malaysian government's revenue collection consisting of 73.2% of the total share. Conversely, the data also indicated a rise in the overall number of cases chosen for tax audits and tax investigations. The report highlighted that

IRBM is committed to performing thorough tax audits and investigations to encourage voluntary compliance and discourage tax evasion.

1.1. Tax Fraud

Several definitions of tax fraud have been developed based on the analysis of prior research. "Intentional illegal behaviours or activities involving a direct violation of tax law to evade the payment of tax" is the definition of tax fraud given by Ameyaw and Dzaka (2016). Tax evasion, according to Azrina Mohd Yusof and Ling Lai (2014), is the practice of reducing one's tax liability by using illicit or fraudulent revenue. Tax evasion, according to Catherine Lynn Burns' new study (2019), is any intentional act of avoiding any imposed tax, including failing to pay such taxes. Certain types of tax avoidance are covered by these several definitions, but not all of them – for example, choosing to take itemised deductions rather than the standard deduction. Since this conduct reduces taxes without violating the letter or the spirit of the law, it is deemed lawful. Under the new definition, improper itemised deductions would be seen as tax evasion and would therefore be criminal or tax fraud (Catherine Lynn Burns, 2019). According to the definition of tax fraud given above, it is crucial to remember that, unlike mistakes or inadvertent misreporting, tax fraud typically involves deliberate and wilful behaviour with the goal of minimising tax liability.

Financial statement fraud is closely associated with tax fraud among various forms of financial fraud since the latter reduces or increases deductible expenses, which in turn impacts the overall revenues of the organisation (Md Noor et al., 2012). The corporation is considered to have committed tax fraud if fraudulent financial reporting is found during the tax audit or investigation procedure.

A financial statement serves as a key tool for figuring out how much taxes a business must pay. On the other hand, to reduce total tax liabilities, fraudulent financial statements may overestimate purchases, assets, sales, and profits while understating costs, liabilities, or losses (Zakaria et al., 2013). Managers may be incentivised to manipulate earnings higher by tax incentives that lower taxable income or by accounting-based contracts such as debt covenants and incentive plans (Shackelford & Shevlin, 2001). Regardless of whether earnings management aims to raise or lower reported earnings, other research by Badertscher et al. (2006) revealed that businesses typically controlled earnings in ways that minimised their cost of tax on current income.

In other circumstances, businesses disclose to shareholders and tax authorities various amounts of income. According to Desai's (2005) research, American businesses kept two distinct sets of financial statements: one set declared "book profits", while the other set reported "tax profits" to tax authorities. Managers were therefore able to misclassify tax savings to capital markets and profits to tax authorities by using two distinct sets of financial statements. This lowers the company's tax liability and has an impact on the financial statement of the company.

2. Tax Audit and Tax Investigation Activities of the Inland Revenue Board of Malaysia (IRBM)

Given the prevalence of tax fraud, the tax authority primarily relies on tax audit and tax investigation activities as the principal enforcement tactics carried out by the IRBM. Their objectives are to provide education and enhance taxpayers' understanding of their rights and obligations as outlined in the ITA 1967, while also discouraging instances of tax fraud (IRBM, 2022). If, during the audit process, it is found that there has been a deliberate understatement or omission of income for the purpose of tax evasion, a penalty will be levied in accordance with paragraph 113(2) of the Income Tax Act.

IRBM has strengthened its tax audit and investigation activities as part of its efforts to better its enforcement strategy and combat tax fraud (Prabowo et al., 2022). Both tasks are carried out by distinctive departments, specifically the Tax Audit and Tax Investigation Department. As a result, in January 2007, the IRBM released the Tax Audit Framework to address the need for a more transparent and efficient tax audit. This framework provides guidance to taxpayers, tax auditors, and tax agents/representatives on the procedures involved in conducting a tax audit. Afterwards, the IRBM made multiple revisions to the Tax Audit Framework to guarantee that tax audits are carried out with fairness, transparency, and impartiality. The most recent framework was amended in May 2022.

As indicated in the Tax Audit Framework, "The primary goal of tax audit is to ensure that a higher tax compliance rate is achieved under the self-assessment system and to encourage voluntary compliance with the tax laws and regulations" (IRBM, 2022). In particular, tax audits involve looking over a taxpayer's business records and paperwork to make sure the correct amount of revenue is reported, and taxes paid comply with tax rules and regulations. Educating taxpayers and raising their awareness of their rights and obligations under the terms of the Income Tax Act are further objectives of tax audit activity.

IRBM conducts two types of tax audits: desk audits and field audits. The desk audit is performed at IRBM's office, utilising the documents (such as the annual return) provided by the taxpayers. On the other hand, the field audit takes place at the taxpayer's business premises. Respective taxpayers will receive a notification letter informing them about the tax audit visit and providing a list of the relevant documents required. The likelihood of a taxpayer being chosen for a tax audit occurs once every five years, according to the IRBM (2019). Any discrepancies discovered during the audit will result in charges under either Section 113 for filing an erroneous return or Section 114 for wilful evasion, as stipulated in the Income Tax Act of 1967.

Furthermore, as outlined in the Tax Audit Framework, the selection of taxpayers for auditing is carried out through either a computerised system that analyses risks, or by targeting specific industries and business locations. Alternatively, taxpayers may be selected based on specific issues related to a particular type of taxpayer, or based on information provided by third parties, such as whistle-blowers. Once the tax audit begins, the settlement should be completed within a period of three months. If the audit case requires more time, the IRBM will inform the taxpayer about the progress and status of the audit. Regarding tax penalties, the framework specifies that if the audit uncovers any instances of underreporting or omission of income after the audit has begun, a penalty will be imposed under subsection 113(2) of the Income Tax Act. This penalty will be equal to 100% of the amount of tax that was undercharged.

In addition to the Tax Audit Framework, which went into effect on January 1, 2007, IRBM also released the Tax Investigation Framework, which aims to inform taxpayers about the laws pertaining to tax investigations, help them fulfil their obligations, and give guidelines regarding the rights and responsibilities of tax officers, who carry out the investigations. In a similar vein, the Tax Investigation Framework has also undergone revisions; the most recent version was released on January 1, 2023. In contrast to a tax audit, a tax investigation necessitates a more thorough review of all the taxpayer's documents, books, records, items, articles, and other materials pertaining to their business and financial affairs, including personal records, to make sure the amount of income reported and paid is accurate and compliant with tax laws and regulations. Only when there is substantial evidence of deliberate tax avoidance and evasion is a tax investigation launched.

The right of tax officers to carry out their duties (i.e. tax investigation activities) is further emphasised by the Tax Investigation Framework. For example, Section 79 grants the right to a statement of the accounts; Section 80 grants access to taxpayers' facilities and papers; and Section 81 grants the right to further information requests. For instance, Section 80 gives tax officers complete and unrestricted access to all taxpayers' assets, including their lands, buildings, and other locations, as well as any other papers pertinent to their investigational duties. Moreover, this clause can be enforced without a warrant. In addition, the director general of IRBM is authorised by Section 81 to demand that anyone provide any information or details needed to support the inquiry, either verbally or in writing. Comparable to a field audit (or tax audit), there is a good chance that an unexpected visit could be conducted to gather enough documentation and data about tax investigation cases.

Tax investigations can be classified into two categories: criminal tax investigations and civil tax investigations. While the latter focuses on gathering evidence and support to prosecute the tax evader or tax fraudster under the Penal Code and related criminal acts, tax investigations aim to detect tax fraud with the primary goal of recovering tax losses and imposing significant penalties (IRBM, 2020). Furthermore, the ITA is not the only statute that contains provisions pertaining to tax investigations; other acts that fall under the purview of the IRBM authority include the Real Property Gains Tax Act of 1967, the Petroleum (Income Tax) Act of 1967, the Promotion of Investment Act of 1986, the Stamp Act of 1949, and the Labuan Offshore Business Activity Tax Act of 1990. The right of tax officers to carry out their duties (i.e. tax investigation activities) is further emphasised by the "Tax Investigation Framework".

For example, Section 79 grants the right to a statement of the accounts; Section 80 grants access to taxpayers' facilities and papers; and Section 81 grants the right to further information requests. For instance, Section 80 gives tax officers complete and unrestricted access to all taxpayers' assets, including their lands, buildings, and other locations, as well as any other papers pertinent to their investigational duties. Moreover, this clause can be enforced without a warrant. In addition, the director general of IRBM is authorised by Section 81 to demand that anyone provide any information or details needed to support the inquiry, either verbally or in writing. Comparable to a field audit (or tax audit), there is a good chance that an unexpected visit could be conducted to gather enough documentation and data about tax investigation cases.

2.1. The Roles of Tax Auditors and Tax Investigators

Tax officers (tax auditors and tax investigators) bear significant responsibilities in identifying tax fraud when they carry out tax audits and investigation duties (OECD, 2017). In the case of IRBM, the tax officers of the IRBM have a crucial function in the implementation of Malaysian tax legislation. They serve as the primary representatives of IRBM, as their job entails engaging and managing taxpayers during tax audits or investigations. The main responsibility of tax officers is to identify and prevent tax evasion by conducting thorough investigations of taxpayers' financial records and interpreting intricate laws and regulations (Bahl & Bird, 2008; OECD, 2017). In addition, they wield significant discretionary authority and often function as both prosecutors and adjudicators in tax assessment proceedings (Isa & Pope, 2011; Muhammad, 2013). Tax officers have the responsibility of examining taxpayers' records and documents, but they also need to interpret intricate tax laws and conduct thorough examinations of taxpayers' books and records (Isa & Pope, 2011; OECD, 2017).

Tax officers are assigned different duties; therefore, they must be equipped with auditing skills in addition to technical and tacit knowledge. According to Bahl and Bird (2008), tax officers face greater difficulties and problems because of globalisation in the new millennium, which requires them to be extremely knowledgeable about the various tax system structures. These involve figuring out the exact tax amount utilising an appropriate audit plan and techniques and comprehending the business intents of taxpayers. Moreover, tax officers may have challenges when dealing with situations that blur the line between tax fraud and acceptable tax avoidance. One such challenge is the absence of audit evidence caused by using paperless systems in the commercial operations of taxpayers (Noch et al., 2022).

In carrying out their duties, tax officials should, in general, not have a significant stake in any organisations; if they do, they should transfer their control to a third party. Therefore, to prevent a conflict of interest, tax officers are not allowed to work on tax audits or investigations for organisations that are controlled or owned by their family members or other individuals with whom they have a close personal relationship (Kasipillai & Chen, 2014). Additionally, in order to prevent misbehaviour by any parties during the tax audit or inquiry process, tax officials are not permitted to conduct audits on their own. Regarding this, tax authorities typically provide tax officers with a code of ethics to ensure that the tax audit process is conducted in a professional manner.

The IRBM tax officers are regulated by the Tax Officers' Guidelines and Work Ethics as a general work ethics procedure. The guidelines are shown in Table 1.

Table 1. The IRBM Tax Officers' Guidelines and Work Ethics

Dos	Don'ts
Honest, diligent, trustworthy, discipline, and responsible	Corruption and any dubious act
Professional, efficient and committed in providing a fair and quality service	Conduct any act that may conflict with organisation interest
Vigilant to the changes related to the profession	Abuse of power
	Extreme involvement in any activities outside the scope of IRBM's core affairs
Continue learning	Conduct any act that may emphasise self-interest and ignore the public duty
Helpful, tolerance with no discrimination and team spirit	Conduct any discreditable act to the organisation
Innovative and creative to enhance the quality service	Involvement in gambling and misconduct
Consistent improvement of quality and productivity	Disobey the superior's instructions
Give priority to organisation's interest by adapting to the task assigned	
Keep secret the confidentiality of the Government and organisational materials	

Tax officers are required to follow the guidelines in the tax audit or investigation framework when carrying out their duties as tax auditors or investigators. The framework has specified that they must be courteous, professional, trustworthy, honest, and uphold their integrity. They also need to be prepared to provide clear explanations of the goals of tax audits and investigations, as well as the rights and responsibilities of taxpayers (Chalu & Mzee, 2018). They also need to be knowledgeable and fair in the administration of tax laws, cooperative and prepared to offer taxpayers guidance, and able to explain proposed tax adjustments and give taxpayers enough time to respond to audit issues. Finally, they need to ensure that taxpayers' rights and interests, as well as the documents they own, are protected.

3. Tax Fraud Risk Judgment

Tax officers are also subjected to risk assessment, particularly in tax fraud risk. In performing the tax audit or investigation, tax officers are required to exercise their judgment throughout the audit or investigation process by assessing taxpayer's business records and financial affairs (i.e. financial statements) to determine the right amount of income declared and the amount of tax calculated and paid is in accordance with tax laws and regulations IRBM (2019, 2020). Specifically, in accordance with the provision of section 90 (2) of the Income Tax Act 1967, a tax officer is demanded to make judgment based on a taxpayer's estimated income. For instance, tax officers make judgment to perform further investigation or do additional testing if they have the opinion that the submitted annual return form has been calculated wrongly (e.g. the net assets accumulated over a period did not match with the income returned for that period), there is a dispute over the taxability of a certain income source (i.e. gains from rental income held to be taxable under section 4(a) of Business Income or section 4(d) of Rental Income of the Income Tax Act 1967 as both types of income have a different method of tax calculation.

However, several factors must be considered before tax officers make a decision. These include the amount of income assessed in the prior year or years, the type and size of the taxpayer's business, the average rate of profit made by taxpayers operating in the same locality, and any specific information that tax officers may have access to (Muhammadi et al., 2016). Tax officers must appropriately assess fraud risk to avoid performing needless audit work, as doing so could impact the audit or investigation's overall budget; alternatively, they must conduct enough audit work to run the risk of failing to find a significant or material misstatement (Krambia-Kapardis et al., 2010). Due to the fast expansion of business and the complexity of transactions, tax officers are now expected to perform substantially higher levels of assurance about financial fraud (Trotman, 2006).

A lower tax risk assessment rating could result in fewer documents being examined closely and recommendations to end an audit or probe without triggering a tax adjustment or penalty. On the other hand, a greater tax risk rating could need a more extensive and comprehensive audit, more audit procedures, larger findings, and higher taxes to be assessed against the taxpayers (Onuoha & Dada, 2016). However, it should be noted that this routine only defines a portion of the JDM process; in actuality, many other components interact, including human-automation interaction, the ability to respond to alarms and warnings, the support of technological aid, error mitigation, and the decision-makers cognitive abilities (Mosier & Fischer, 2018).

The IRBM Tax Audit and Tax Investigation Framework's rules and procedures, as well as the Income Tax Act of 1967's regulations, serve as a reference for tax officers in their subjective assessment of tax fraud risk. This is not an easy assignment to complete. As a result, tax officials must use their judgment while making decisions by considering pertinent external factors (Muhammad, 2013). They must determine the level of potential tax fraud risk, make a decision about what to do next, and, if needed, seek additional information and clarification from the relevant parties (such as the taxpayer's organisation's top management, their tax consultant, or their tax agent). Tax officers' decisions and behavioural aspects play a significant role in mitigating tax fraud situations; thus, they merit consideration. Since tax officers play a pivotal role in determining the likelihood of tax fraud, their tax fraud risk judgment is influenced by both their personal conduct and the external factors surrounding them, such as the workplace environment and the context of their work setting.

4. Conclusion

Given the complexity of tax fraud, tax officers are expected to have unique traits and competency in determining the risk of tax fraud that align with the appropriate degree of judgment to guarantee that the risk is appropriately addressed (IRBM, 2022, 2021; ISA 200, 2009; ISA 240, 2018). Tax officers' inherent capacity to overcome challenges in conducting tax audits during fieldwork is demonstrated by their scepticism and competent attitude in using sound professional judgment. It would be difficult for the tax officers to fully evaluate the client's risk of tax fraud if they lacked the necessary skills and knowledge to carry out their duties (Fullerton & Durtschi, 2005; Popova, 2013; Quadackers et al., 2014).

In conducting tax audit and tax investigation tasks, tax officers must have up-to-date knowledge of tax accounting, determining tax compliance, financial analysis skills, effective communication, technical expertise of tax law and applying audit processes and procedures. On top of that, the tax officers are emphasised with the needs of "soft skills" and other attributes for tax officers such as a passion for work and integrity, intention to detect fraud and irregularities, observing and detecting relevant indicators in the surroundings and identifying patterns and describing their significance to the current situation, which requires observation skills. Tax officers should also have appropriate knowledge of basic accounting, bookkeeping, business and industry practices (Muhammad & Salikin, 2013).

The roles of tax auditors and tax investigators are of paramount importance in the battle against tax fraud, with profound implications for government revenue and the ability to provide essential facilities to nations. These professionals serve as the frontline defenders of a fair and equitable tax system (Salehi et al., 2020). Their efforts not only detect and prevent tax fraud but also contribute to the overall well-being of a nation's economy and public trust in the tax system.

Tax auditors and investigators play a pivotal role in safeguarding government revenue. By meticulously scrutinising financial records and transactions, they uncover instances of tax evasion and underreporting. This detection results in the recovery of funds owed to the government, subsequently increasing government revenue. The additional revenue can be channelled into critical areas such as healthcare, education, infrastructure, and social services, ultimately enhancing the quality of life for citizens (Irawan & Utama, 2021). Moreover, combating tax fraud through effective audits and investigations ensures the accuracy of economic statistics and the proper allocation of resources. When economic data is reliable, policymakers can make informed decisions that support sustainable economic growth. The misallocation of resources is minimised, and market incentives are preserved, promoting a healthier and more robust economy.

Acknowledgement

The authors would like to extend their gratitude to the Accounting Research Institute, HiCOE and Universiti Teknologi MARA for funding this research under the Bestari Grant – Islamic Financial Criminology, with reference number 600-RMC/DANA 5/3/BESTARI (TD) (010/2022)

References

Alleyne, P., & Howard, M. (2005). An exploratory study of auditors' responsibility for fraud detection in Barbados. *Managerial Auditing Journal, 20*(3), 284–303.

Association of Certified Fraud Examiners. (2022). *Report to the nation's 2022 Global Fraud Study.*

Ameyaw, B., & Dzaka, D. (2016). Determinants of tax evasion: Empirical evidence from Ghana. *Modern Economy*, 1653–1664.

Bailey, C. D. (2004). An unusual cash control procedure. *Journal of Accounting Education, 22*(2), 119–129.

Badertscher, B., Phillips, J., Pincus, M., & Rego, S. O. (2006). *Tax implications of earnings management activities: Evidence from restatements.* Merage School of Business, University of California.

Bahl, R. W., & Bird, R. M. (2008). Tax policy in developing countries: Looking back and forward. *National Tax Journal, 61*(2), 279–301.

Bedard, J. C., & Graham, L. (2002). The effects of risk decision aid orientation on risk factor identification and audit test planning. *A Journal of Practice & Theory, 21*(2), 39–56.

Blay, A. D., Kizirian, T., & Sneathen, L. D. (2007). The effects of fraud and going-concern risk on auditors' assessment of the risk of material misstatement and resulting audit procedures'. *International Journal of Auditing, 11*(3), 149–163.

Borck, R. (2004). Stricter enforcement may increase tax evasion. *European Journal of Political Economy, 20*(3), 725–737.

Brazel, J. F., Carpenter, T. D., & Jenkins, J. G. (2010). Auditors' use of brainstorming in the consideration of fraud: Reports from the field. *The Accounting Review, 85*(4), 1273–1301.

Catherine Lynn Burns. (2019). *Personality in fraud model constructs: Characterizing potential tax fraud perpetrators* (Issue July). Northcentral University.

Chalu, H., & Mzee, H. (2018). Determinants of tax audit effectiveness in Tanzania. *Managerial Auditing Journal, 33*(1).

Desai, M. A. (2005). *The degradation of reported corporate profits.* Harvard University.

Dezoort, T., & Harrison, P. (2008). *An evaluation of internal auditor responsibility for fraud detection.* The Institute of Internal Auditors Research Foundation.

Favere-Marchesi, M. (2006). The impact of tax services on auditors' fraud-risk assessment. *Advances in Accounting, 22*(06), 149–165.

Irawan, F., & Utama, A. S. (2021). The impact of tax audit and corruption perception on tax evasion. *International Journal of Business and Society, 22*(3), 1158–1173.

Inland Revenue Board of Malaysia (IRBM). (1999). Panduan dan Etika Kerja. IRBM. (2017). IRBM Annual Report 2017. IRBM. (2019). Tax Audit Framework.https://www.irbm.com/wp-content/uploads/IRBM_Code_of_Ethics_EN.pdf

Inland Revenue Board of Malaysia (IRBM). (2022). *Annual report.*

Inland Revenue Board of Malaysia. (2020). *Tax investigation framework.* https://phl.hasil.gov.my/pdf/pdfam/Tax_Investigation_Framework_2020_2.pdf

ISA 200. (2009). *International standard on auditing 200: Overall objectives of the independent auditor and the conduct of an audit in accordance with international standards on auditing* (pp. 72–100). http://www.ifac.org/sites/default/files/publications/files/2012%20IAASB%20Handbook%20Part%20I_Web.pdf

Isa, K., & Pope, J. (2011). Corporate tax audits: Evidence from Malaysia. *Global Review of Accounting and Finance, 2*(1), 42–56.

Kasipillai, J., & Chen, L. E. (2014). Relevant areas for research to gain insight into taxation issues – MTRF report.

Krambia-Kapardis, M., Christodoulou, C., & Agathocleous, M. (2010). Neural networks: The panacea in fraud detection? *Managerial Auditing Journal, 25*(7), 659–678.

Lai, M. L., Yaacob, Z., Omar, N., Abdul Aziz, N., & Yap, B. W. (2013). Examining corporate tax evaders: Evidence from the finalized audit cases. *International Journal of Social, Economics and Management Engineering, 7*(6), 615–619.

Libby, R., & Luft, J. (1993). Determinants of judgement performance in accounting settings: Ability, knowledge, motivation, and environment. *Accounting, Organizations and Society, 18*(5), 425–450.

Md Noor, R., Aziz, A. A., Mastuki, N., & Ismail, N. (2012). Tax fraud indicators. *Malaysia Accounting Review, 11*(1), pp. 43–57.

Miskam, M., Md Noor, R., Omar, N., Abd Aziz, R. (2013). Determinants of tax evasion on imported vehicles. In *Procedia economics and finance* (Vol. 7, pp. 205–212). Elsevier B.V.

Mohamad, A., Zakaria, M. H., & Hamid, Z. (2016). Cash economy: Tax evasion amongst SMEs in Malaysia. *Journal of Financial Crime, 23*(4), 974–986.

Mosier, K. L., & Fischer, U. M. (2018). Judgement and decision making by individuals and teams: Issues, models, and applications. *Decision Making in Aviation*, (July), 139–198.

Muhammad, I. (2013). An exploratory study of Malaysian tax auditors' enforcement regulatory styles. *Procedia Economics and Finance*, 188–196.

Muhammadi, A. H., Ahmed, Z., & Habib, A., (2016). Multinational transfer pricing of intangible assets: Indonesian tax auditors' perspectives. *Asian Review of Accounting*, 24(3).

Ngah, Z. A., Ismail, N., & Abd Hamid, N. (2022). A cohesive model of predicting tax evasion from the perspective of fraudulent financial reporting amongst small and medium-sized enterprises. *Accounting Research Journal*, 35(3), 349–363.

Noch, M. Y., Ibrahim, M. B. H., Akbar, M. A., Kartim, K., & Sutisman, E. (2022). Independence and competence on audit fraud detection: Role of professional scepticism as moderating. *Jurnal Akuntansi*, 26(1), 161–175.

OECD. (2017). *Strengthening tax audit capabilities: General principles and approaches.*

Onuoha, L. N., & Dada, S. O. (2016). Tax audit and investigation as imperatives for efficient tax administration in Nigeria. *Journal of Business Administration and Management Sciences Research*, 5(5), 66–076.

Prabowo, R., Sucahwo, U., Damayanti, T., & Supramono, S. (2022). Tax enforcement and private firms' audited financial statements: The moderating role of secrecy culture. *Journal of Accounting in Emerging Economies*, 12(3).

Salehi, M., Tarighi, H., & Shahri, T. A. (2022). The effect of auditor characteristics on tax avoidance of Iranian companies. *Journal of Asian Business and Economic Studies*, 27(2).

Shackelford, D. A., & Shevlin, T. (2001). Empirical tax research in accounting. *Journal of Accounting & Economics*, 31, 321–387.

Trotman, K. (2006). *Professional judgement: Are auditors being held to a higher standard than other professionals?*

Wilks, T. J., & Zimbelman, M. F. (2004). Decomposition of fraud risk assessments and auditors' sensitivity to fraud cues. *Contemporary Accounting Research*, 21(3), 719–745.

Zakaria, M., Ahmad, J. H., & Wan Mohamad Noor, W. N. B. (2013). Tax evasion: A financial crime rationalized? *Scientific Research Journal* (SCIRJ), 1(2), 3–6.

Fazlida Mohd Razali, Jamaliah Said, & Razana Juhaida Johari

Empowering Organisations Through Confident Risk Navigation: The Crucial Role of Internal Auditors

1. Introduction

Numerous incidents of continuous corporate collapses caused by fiduciary neg-ligence of corporate governance actors have led to diminishing public trust on the overall corporate governance system. Internal auditors, which is one of the key corporate governance actors, have recently come under criticism for failing to discharge their responsibilities diligently (Chambers, 2015). This has been evidenced by the revelation of scandals of well-known conglomerate, Toshiba, in a case of overstated profit by USD $1.8 billion, and Silver Bird Berhad, in a case of falsification of invoices worth RM64.7 million. Increasing number of litigation suits filed against internal auditor has proved that expectations from stakeholders and heightened scrutiny are mounting when things go wrong (Leech, 2017). In both Toshiba and Silver Bird Berhad scandals, the internal auditors were accused of failing to assess the existence of accounting irregularities and fraud risk, leading to fraud becoming undetected and eventually huge losses and damage to the reputation of the two companies. In other words, the failure of the internal auditors to appropriately apply risk judgment could lead to audit failure and significant bad consequences to the company. This has apparently raised a question of whether risk judgment is critical for the success of overall internal audit process. This chapter delves into the intricate definition of risk judgment and its profound implications for the overarching internal audit process. It also provides a comprehensive discussion on the standards that are applicable to an internal auditor's exercise of risk judgment. Furthermore, it underscores the critical significance of risk judgment within the broader framework of governance. Finally, this chapter sheds light on emerging risks that demand the immediate and focused attention of internal auditors.

2. Internal Auditor Judgment

2.1. Definition of Judgment

From an academic perspective, Bonner (1999) defined judgment as "an idea, opinion, or estimate about an object, an event, a state, or another type of phenomenon". From a professional point of view, Wedemeyer (2010) defined audit judgment as "description of any decision or evaluation made by auditor, which influences or governs the process and outcome of an audit of financial statement". More precisely, judgment is defined under Para 16 of International Standard of Auditing 200 or ISA 200 as "the application of relevant training, knowledge and experience, within the context provided by auditing and ethical standards, in making informed decision about the courses of action that are appropriate in the circumstances of the audit engagement".

International Standards for the Professional Practice of Internal Auditing (ISPPIA) does not precisely define judgment. However, the ISPPIA states that while conformance to the Standard is expected, one's judgment might differ depending on the circumstances. The ISPPIA justify the differences between the use of word "must" and "should" in the Standard. The ISPPIA specifically states that the use of word "should" means conformance, which is expected unless when applying professional judgment, circumstances justify deviation. Both internal and external audit professional standards emphasise the important of professional judgment to be exercised throughout the entire auditing process (Trotman et al., 2011). The auditing process is described as a sequence of processes (Bamber, 1980), which require auditors to exercise their professional judgment. Figure 1 depicts the internal control audit process as proposed by Asare et al. (2013).

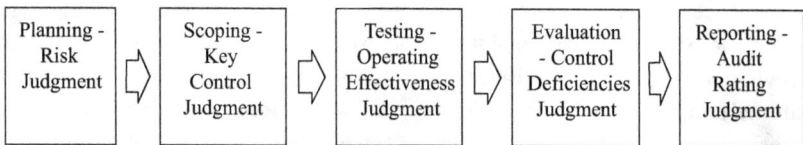

Planning - Risk Judgment		Scoping - Key Control Judgment		Testing - Operating Effectiveness Judgment		Evaluation - Control Deficiencies Judgment		Reporting - Audit Rating Judgment

Figure 1. Internal Control Audit Process

Each stage of the audit process requires auditors to exercise their professional judgment to enable them to proceed to the next stage (ISA 200: A27). Among the judgments involved in internal audit process include risk judgment, key control judgment, operating effectiveness judgment, control deficiencies judgment and audit rating judgment (Asare et al., 2013). The performance of judgment made in the latter stage is highly dependent on the judgment made in the earlier stages (ISA 200: A23). For instance, internal auditor's judgment on key risk areas will determine the auditable area that they will focus on to give an overall judgment on operating effectiveness and control deficiencies. The flaws in internal auditor's risk judgment at planning stage will result in the flaws of the overall opinion audit process.

The ISPPIA does not have a specific paragraph for professional judgment. However, consistent with the auditing process depicted in Figure 1, the Standard does emphasise the need to apply professional judgment throughout the audit process. In general, ISPPIA highlights the importance of judgment in identifying matters significant to the audit especially at planning stage (ISPPIA: Para 2010); testing and assessing operating effectiveness (ISPPIA: Para 2120); and overall opinion on conclusion reach (ISPPIA: Para 2420). Overall, the quality of the entire audit process depends on the judgment made in each of the audit stages.

2.2. Internal Auditor's Risk Judgment

Risk is defined as "the possibility of an event occurring that will have an impact on the achievement of objectives" (IIA, 2016). Meanwhile, judgment as discussed above is "an idea, opinion, or estimate about an object, an event, a state, or another type of phenomenon" (Bonner, 1999). Thus, in the context of this study, risk judgment is defined as "an opinion or estimated possibility of event occurring that will have an impact on the achievement of objectives". Rapid changes in today's business environment and the associated risks demand internal audit to improve risk judgment in order to satisfy multi-stakeholder's need (Leech, 2017). This notion is well communicated by "Institute of Internal Auditors Malaysia" (herein IIAM) through the mission of that professional institutes which aim to enhance and protect organisational value by providing risk-based and objective assurance, advice and insight (Rittenberg, 2015). In line with the mission, there is a growing adoption of Risk-based Internal Audit (RBIA) approach by Internal Audit Function (IAF) in Malaysia (Abidin, 2017).

Table 1. List of ISPPIA's Paragraphs on Risk Judgment

Para	Details
1210: Proficiency	
1210.A2	Internal auditors must have sufficient knowledge to evaluate the risk of fraud and the manner in which it is managed by the organisation, but are not expected to have the expertise of a person whose primary responsibility is detecting and investigating fraud.
1210.A3	Internal auditors must have sufficient knowledge of key information technology risks and controls and available technology-based audit techniques to perform their assigned work.
1220: Professional Due Care	
1220.A3	Internal auditors must be alert to the significant risks that might affect objectives, operations, or resources. However, assurance procedures alone, even when performed with due professional care, do not guarantee that all significant risks will be identified.
2010: Planning	
2010	The CAE must establish a risk-based plan to determine the priorities of the internal audit activity, consistent with the organisation's goals.
2010.A1	The internal audit activity's plan of engagement must be based on a documented risk assessment, undertaken at least annually. The input from senior management and the board must be considered in this process.
2010.C1	The CAE should consider accepting proposed consulting engagements based on the engagement's potential to improve management of risks, add value, and improve the organisation's operations. Accepted engagements must be included in the plan.
2060: Reporting to Senior Management and the Board	
2060	The CAE must report periodically to senior management and the board on internal audit activity's purpose, authority, responsibility, and performance relative to its plan and on its conformance with the Code of Ethics and the Standards. Reporting must also include significant risk and control issues, including fraud risks, governance issues, and other matters that require the attention of senior management and/or the board.
2100: Nature of Work	
2100	The internal audit activity must evaluate and contribute to the improvement of the organisation's governance, risk management, and control processes using a systematic, disciplined, and risk-based approach. Internal audit credibility and value are enhanced when auditors are proactive, and their evaluations offer new insights and consider future impact.

Para	Details
2120: Risk Management	
2120	The internal audit activity must evaluate the effectiveness and contribute to the improvement of risk management processes.
2120.A1	The internal audit activity must evaluate risk exposures relating to the organisation's governance, operations, and information systems regarding the achievement of the organisation's strategic objectives, reliability and integrity of financial and operational information, effectiveness and efficiency of operations and programmes, safeguarding of assets and compliance with laws, regulations, policies, procedures, and control.
2120.A2	The internal audit activity must evaluate the potential for the occurrence of fraud and how the organisation manages fraud risk.
2120.C1	During consulting engagements, internal auditors must address risk consistent with the engagement's objectives and be alert to the existence of other significant risks.
2120.C2	Internal auditors must incorporate knowledge of risks gained from consulting engagements into their evaluation of the organisation's risk management processes.
2120.C3	When assisting management in establishing or improving risk management processes, internal auditors must refrain from assuming any management responsibility by managing risks.
2130.A1	The internal audit activity must evaluate the adequacy and effectiveness of controls in responding to risks within the organisation's governance, operations, and information systems.

Source: IPPF: International Standards for Professional Practices on Internal Auditing (IIA, 2016, pp. 6–14)

Based on the relevant paragraphs listed in Table 1, it is crucial for an internal auditor to possess sufficient level of proficiency and professional due care to enable them to foresee existing and emerging risks that could threaten the organisation's governance, operations, and reliability and integrity of financial and operational information (IIA, 2016). An internal auditor's risk judgment ability is important to meet the core requirement of professional practices for internal auditing especially in preparing the annual risk-based internal audit plan and giving an assurance on the effectiveness of risk management process in the organisation. As an agent to multi-stakeholders, it is vital that an internal auditor exercises the highest quality of risk judgment. Internal auditor's risk judgment is highly relied upon by multi-stakeholders to form their judgment on critical business decision. To create value, internal auditors are expected to have the ability to form judgments on risks that matter to the boards and management (Leech, 2017; Marks, 2017; Seago, 2015).

3. The Importance of Internal Auditor's Risk Judgment

Internal audit became a more visible component of corporate governance in Malaysia when it was made mandatory beginning 31 January 2009, for a listed company to have an internal audit function. Internal audit, as the third line of defence, is an integral part of an effective organisational corporate governance (Christ et al., 2015). As illustrated in Figure 1, internal auditor is accountable to multi-stakeholders, namely governing body (Board of Directors [BODs] and Audit Committees [AC]), Regulator, External Auditor and Senior Management. Each of the stakeholders has different needs to be fulfilled by internal auditor.

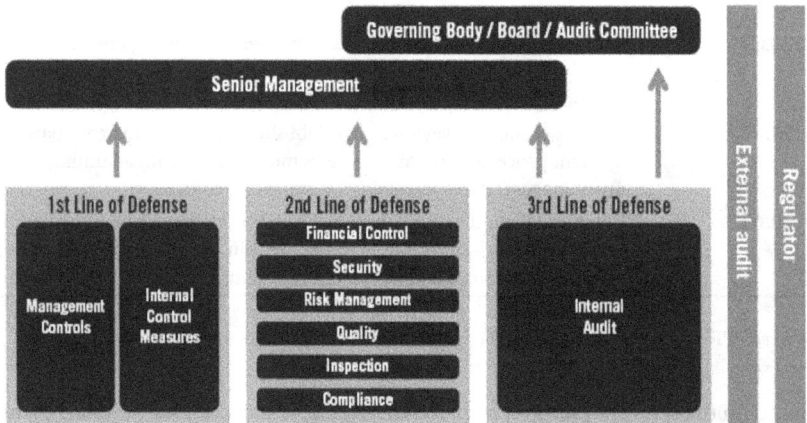

Figure 2. The Three Lines of Defence
Source: IIA Position Paper: The Three Lines of Defence in Effective Risk Management and Control (IIA, 2013, p. 2)

The importance of risk judgment is clearly stated in ISPPIA, particularly in the planning stage, where the Chief Audit Executive (CAE) is required by Para 2010 to establish a risk-based plan to direct the internal audit activity (IIA, 2016). CAE would usually depend on the input from the risk judgment made by subordinates. The expertise of both (Para 1210.A2) the CAE and the internal audit staff members in forming a sound risk judgment will determine the result of risk assessment exercise which is undertaken at least once a year. Specifically, Para

1220.A3 states that an internal auditor "must be alert of significant risk affecting the objectives, the operation and resources" (IIA, 2016, p. 7), be it the existing risk or emerging risk (Ibrahim, 2016; KPMG, 2008; Soh & Martinov-Bennie, 2011).

There is a growing adoption of RBIA that is consistent with the requirement of the Standards which would require internal auditors to make a holistic judgment on risk (Robson et al., 2007). From the Standards setter's point of view, risk-based audit not only improves auditors' knowledge about the company risk but indirectly helps to increase audit quality (Messier, 2014). Meanwhile, Audit Committee Chairman and CAE are of opinion that the role played by internal auditors in the risk is becoming more significant (Soh & Martinov-Bennie, 2011). It has been found that internal audit function has evolved from "ticking the box" audit to more value-added, risk-based audit. This is consistent with the findings of Sarens et al. (2012), which confirmed that internal audit functions have added value to organisation governance through the use of risk-based audit plans. Hence, internal auditor's risk judgment performance is crucial not only for compliance with ISPPIA but also to create value for the organisation via RBIA.

As an agent to multi-stakeholders, it is vital that an internal auditor exercises the highest quality of risk judgment. Para 15.26 (b) of Bursa Malaysia Listing Requirement mandated BODs to disclose the statement of risk management and internal control (BMSB, 2018) in their annual report. BODs rely on internal auditor's risk judgment to enable them to conclude that the risk faced by the organisation has been properly identified, managed and controlled (IIAM, 2015). BODs also depend on internal audit to evaluate the effectiveness of the governance, risk management, and internal control framework. Furthermore, Malaysian Code of Corporate Governance (MCCG) spells out the crucial role of internal audit as the main source to AC (SCM, 2017) which is to conduct assurance activities on behalf of AC (Boyle et al., 2015) especially in identification of control deficiencies resulting from risk judgment exercise undertaken.

External auditors are allowed under ISA 610 to use the work of internal auditors. As internal auditor practices RBIA, external auditor uses of internal auditor work depend so much on internal auditor abilities to appropriately apply risk judgment. The President of the IIAM stated that Key Audit Matters (KAM) is one of the high-risk areas that should be addressed by internal auditors (The Star, 2016b). Internal auditor is in the best position to help external auditor to comply with ISA requirements of KAM. As an insider, internal auditor has direct access to company's resources and expertise. Indirectly, uses of internal auditor's work can enhance the external auditor's understanding of the entity and its environment and identification and assessment of the risk of material misstatement (IAASB, 2013a).

As internal auditor's risk judgment is highly relied upon by multi-stakeholders, it is crucial to ensure that the risk judgment is of high quality. The flaws in internal auditor's risk judgment will result in the flaws in the judgment made by multi-stakeholders (i.e. external auditor) (Brody et al., 2015). For instance, internal auditor's failure to accurately apply risk judgment will indirectly mislead the BODs assertion in statement of risk management and internal control especially in terms of internal control effectiveness. Obviously, stakeholders in other countries have started to scrutinise and have taken a drastic action towards internal auditor (i.e. legal action towards Toshiba, Olympus), yet in Malaysia, Silver Bird is the only case.

The revelation of the scandal involving both public and private sector organisations has increased the public scrutiny on the role played by internal auditors as independent assurers in an organisation. The most alarming scandal includes the embezzlement of RM38.5 million federal fund by Senior Officer of Youth Ministry which takes place from February 2012 until November 2015 (The Star, 2016a). Malaysians were profoundly shocked by the revelation of the biggest scandal involving the embezzlement of RM3.3 billion of public money by the director and deputy director of Sabah State Water Department (Astro Awani, 2017).

The public has started to feel curious on how the annual audit conducted by internal audit could miss the misappropriation that has taken place for many years in both the organisations. The revelation of both cases is initiated by tips from third party (i.e. contractor) instead of detected by internal auditor. In both cases, an internal auditor's failure to appropriately apply risk judgment leads to failure in identification of lapse in internal control; thus, allowing the culprit to override all the controls installed. PWC's 2018 Global Economic Crime and Fraud survey stated that only 14% of the most disruptive fraud has been detected by internal auditor (PwC, 2018), which causes the organisation to suffer significant losses. As an agent to multi-stakeholders, this apparently signals a flaw in internal auditor's risk judgment performances which motivate further investigation.

4. Current Issue and Future Research

Growing investor's demand on Environmental, Social and Governance (ESG) reporting might spur organisation desire to disclose extensively without realising the risk of conveying a false impression or providing misleading information about an organisation ESG practices. Recently, there is an intensify public's scrutiny on the extent to which organisation ESG reporting reflects its actual state (Wamsley, 2021). Increase public scrutiny on ESG reporting signals that the company is highly exposed to "ESG Risk". This is supported by recent report by Institute of Internal Auditor "ONRISK 2022" where ESG risk is rated among top 12 risks faced by an organisation in 2022. Rising demand on transparent "ESG Reporting" highlights the crucial need for internal auditor as the "Third Line of Defence" to come into the picture.

To remain relevance, internal auditor's need to play a crucial role in giving an independence assurance on whether ESG risk has been effectively assessed, managed, and controlled by an organisation. As "ESG risk" evolved at the fast-pace, internal auditor, as "risk expert" need to ensure that they play a significant role in organisation ESG journey depending on the maturity of the it's ESG practices. During the preliminary stages of ESG journey, it is crucial for the internal auditor to play a role as "partner" where they play more advisory role. This is especially when there is obvious misalignment between lines of defence on the crucial need to recognise and invest on ESG risk mitigation initiative.

The IIA's ONRISK 2022 report that there is misalignment between C-Suite member, CAE and Board Member views on the significant of ESG Risk to their organisation. This eventually led to low management and BOD buy-in on mitigating ESG risk. Thus, as an adviser, internal auditor should help to educate the Management and BOD on the importance of aligning the ESG towards an organisation overall strategic goal. Notably, the internal auditor should help to coordinate the ESG risk management initiative to ensure that the "tone at the top" are well communicated and executed between line of defence. Along the journey, as ESG become more matured in the organisation, internal auditor should focus more on "assurance role". An independent assurance on ESG risk assessment, response and control could enhance the reliability and transparency which eventually will help to instil public's trust on ESG reporting. Moving forward, to stay relevant, internal auditors must enhance their competency on ESG-related matters to create value for an organisation. According to ONRISK 2022 report (IIA, 2021), only 23% CAE acknowledged having competency in environmental and social sustainability. This apparently called for an urgent move by an individual internal auditor, organisation, and professional bodies especially IIAM. Individual internal auditor's need to upskill to be more competent in ESG. An organisation should encourage their internal auditor to attend more training on ESG. Finally, IIAM, as a body that regulates the profession should take proactive active in enhancing internal auditor's skill and knowledge in ESG through their training and conference. Collectively, this initiative would increase the visibility of the internal audit profession.

5. Conclusion

In today's rapidly evolving business landscape, effective corporate governance has emerged as a cornerstone for sustainable organisational success. With risks becoming more intricate and pervasive, the role of internal auditors has gained importance in ensuring robust corporate governance. This chapter delves into the critical function of internal auditors as navigators of risks employing their expertise to meticulously assess and mitigate a spectrum of risks encompassing financial, operational, and compliance domains. An ability to competently exercise risk judgment will enable internal auditor to effectively evaluate internal controls and processes, provide an unbiased appraisal that aids boards and management in making informed decisions. This indirectly helps to protect an organisation from financial losses, reputational damage, and legal ramifications. This chapter showcases the tangible contributions of internal auditors to long-term sustainability. It highlights how their continuous monitoring and iterative assessments align with the principles of adaptability and resilience that modern corporations must embody. As organisations strive to maintain agility in the face of uncertainty, internal auditors emerge as essential partners in steering corporate strategies toward prudent risk-taking and value creation.

Acknowledgement

The authors would like to extend their gratitude to the Accounting Research Institute, HiCOE and Universiti Teknologi MARA for funding this research under the Bestari Grant – Islamic Financial Criminology, with reference number 600-RMC/DANA 5/3/BESTARI (TD) (010/2022)

References

Abidin, N. H. Z. (2017). Factors influencing the implementation of risk-based auditing. *Asian Review of Accounting, 25*(3), 361–375.

Asare, S. K., Fitzgerald, B. C., Graham, L. E., Joe, J. R., Negangard, E. M., & Wolfe, C. J. (2013). Auditors' internal control over financial reporting decisions: Analysis, synthesis, and research directions. *Auditing: A Journal of Practice & Theory, 32*(October 2012), 131–166.

Astro Awani. (2017). Bekas Timbalan Pengarah Jabatan Air Sabah mengaku tidak bersalah gubah wang haram. *Astro Awani*, p. 1. http://www.astroawani.com/berita-malaysia/bekas-timbalan-pengarah-jabatan-air-sabah-mengaku-tidak-bersalah-gubah-wang-haram-162842

Bamber, E. M. (1980). *Expert judgment in the audit team: An examination of source credibility.* The Ohio State University.

BMSB. (2018). *B. M. S. B. main market listing requirements: Main market.*

Bonner, S. E. (1990). Experience effects in auditing: The role of task-specific knowledge. *The Accounting Review, 65*(1), 72–92.

Boyle, D. M., Dezoort, F. T., & Hermanson, D. R. (2015). The effects of internal audit report type and reporting relationship on internal auditors' risk judgments. *Accounting Horizons, 29*(3), 695–718.

Bonner, S. E. (1990). Experience effects in auditing: The role of task-specific knowledge. *The Accounting Review, 65*(1), 72–92.

Bonner, S. E. (1999). Judgment and decision-making research in accounting. *Accounting Horizons, 13*(4), 385–398.

Brody, R. G., Hayners, C. M., & White, C. G. (2015). Is PCOAB Standard No. 5 impairing auditor objectivity. *Current Issues in Auditing.*

Chambers, R. (2015). *Lessons from Toshiba: When corporate scandals implicate internal audit.* https://iaonline.theiia.org/blogs/chambers/2015/lessons-from-toshiba-when-corporate-scandals-implicate-internal-audit

Christ, M. H., Masli, A., Sharp, N. Y., & Wood, D. A. (2015). Rotational internal audit programs and financial reporting quality: Do compensating controls help? *Accounting, Organizations and Society, 44,* 37–59.

Ibrahim, M. (2016). *Audit as a partner of change.* http://www.bnm.gov.my/index.php?ch=en_speech&pg=en_speech_all&ac=615 &lang=en

IAASB. (2013a). *International auditing and assurance standards board handbook of international quality control, auditing, review, other assurance, and related services pronouncements* (2013 ed., Vol. I).

IIA. (2016). *International standards for the professional practice of internal auditing.* https://scholar.google.com/scholar?q=International+standards+for+the+professional+practice+of+internal+auditing

IIA. (2022). *OnRisk 2022: A guide to understanding, aligning and optimizing risk.* https://www.theiia.org/en/resources/research-and-reports/onrisk/

KPMG. (2008). *The evolving role of the internal auditor: Value creation and preservation from an internal audit perspective.*

Leech, T. (2017). Is internal audit the next blackberry? *Edpacs, 55*(4).

Marks, N. (2017). *What are the biggest risks for internal audit this year and next year?*

Messier, W. F. (2014). An approach to learning risk-based auditing. *Journal of Accounting Education, 32*(3), 276–287.

Rittenberg, L. E. (2015). *Ethics and pressure balancing the internal audit profession.* http://contentz.mkt5790.com/lp/2842/214189/FoundationCBOKEthic sandPressureOct2016V3_0.pdf

Robson, K., Humphrey, C., Khalifa, R., & Jones, J. (2007). Transforming audit technologies: Business risk audit methodologies and the audit field. *Accounting, Organizations and Society, 32*(4–5), 409–438.

SCM. (2017). S. C. M. Malaysian Code of Corporate Governance.

Seago, J. (2015). Delivering on the promise: Measuring internal audit value and performance. *Altamonte Springs.* http://contentz.mkt5790.com/lp/2842/196 909/IIARFCBOKDeliveringonthe PromiseNov2015.pdf

Soh, D. S. B., & Martinov-Bennie, N. (2011). The internal audit function: Perceptions of internal audit roles, effectiveness and evaluation. *Managerial Auditing Journal, 26*(7), 605–622.

PwC. (2018). *Pulling fraud out of the shadows: Global Economic Crime and Fraud Survey 2018.*

The Star. (2016a). Khairy: Immediate review of Youth Ministry's procurement process. *The Star Online.* https://www.thestar.com.my/videos/2016/03/21/kha iry-immediate-review-of-youth-ministrys-procurement-process/

The Star. (2016b, September 19). More work for internal auditors with new standards. *The Star Online,* pp. 1–2. http://www.thestar.com.my/business/busin ess-news/2016/09/19/more-work-for-internal-auditors-with-new-standards/

Trotman, K. T., Tan, H. C., & Ang, N. (2011). Fifty-year overview of judgment and decision-making research in accounting. *Accounting and Finance, 51*(December 2010), 278–360.

Wamsley, L. (2021, October). *ESG reporting: A golden opportunity.* Internal Audit. Retrieved from https://iaonline.theiia.org/2021/Pages/ESG-Report ing-A-Golden-Opportunity.aspx

Wedemeyer, P. D. (2010). A discussion of auditor judgment as the critical component in audit quality – a practitioner's perspective. *International Journal of Disclosure and Governance, 7*(4), 320–333. https://doi.org/10.1057/ jdg.2010.19

Yusarina Mat Isa, Zuraidah Mohd Sanusi, & Muhammad Nazmul Hoque

Theorising Money Laundering Risk Assessment from Behavioural Perspective

1. Introduction

The Financial Action Task Force (FATF) defines money laundering as "the process of disguising criminal proceeds from their illegal origin in order to legitimise the ill-gotten gains of crimes" (FATF, n.d.). In concealing the illegal money, money launderers require a mechanism to transform the money from the illicit origin to make it appears legitimate, such as by using financial intermediaries. The money launderers' motivations in changing the status of the illegal money to clean money are two-fold – to avoid detection of the criminal activities; and, to protect business assets and properties from seizure and forfeiture by the law enforcement authorities (Sarigul, 2013; Shanmugam et al., 2003).

Despite the imperative concern on money laundering risk at the highly exposed institutions – such as banks, insurance companies, and designated non-financial businesses and professions (DNFBPs) – far too little attention has been paid on the behavioural aspect of those personnel involved in the assessment of money laundering risk. Much attention is rather focused on the organisation-based role, for instance, money laundering policies, supervisory control, compliance with the regulatory requirements and other anti-money laundering (AML) issues (Simser, 2013; Simwayi & Wang, 2011). Notwithstanding that these affected institutions put high reliance on automated solutions, such as risk screening system, the human factor in assessing money laundering risk is an important requisite (Cocheo, 2010). Automated solutions are not designed to perform judgment; they can only assist in analysing the situation, thus providing inputs for the personnel to make an informed assessment on the exposure of money laundering risk.

Numerous internal and external factors could have affected money laundering risk assessment, considering that those affected institutions are operating in a dynamic environment. The personnel tasked with the assessment of money laundering risk are often subject to myriad of requirements, both at the individual and institutional levels. In ensuring a robust management of money laundering risk, the affected institutions should consider for both "hard infrastructure" and "soft infrastructure" to be in place. The provision for the hard infrastructure, such as the applications of information technology, availability of screening system and other system infrastructure, is almost an obligatory for most institutions. Huge amount of investment has been set aside for this purpose and this aspect is always on the senior management agenda. However, consideration for soft infrastructure in terms of building human behavioural capability is commonly neglected (Baran & Klos, 2014; Pok et al., 2014). Provisions for soft and hard infrastructures should complement as one always in need of the other in order to fully optimise the personnel capabilities.

This chapter will present three theoretical foundations in supporting the assertions of behavioural perspective for money laundering risk assessment, that is, behavioural decision theory, Bonner's judgment and decision-making (JDM) framework, and modified Simon's model on money laundering risk assessment. This chapter intends to present these three theoretical foundations as a hybrid model that could explain how a personnel's judgment in assessing money laundering risk could have been affected by the factors surrounding them, including the internal and external factors. The hybrid model would signify a more holistic approach for money laundering risk assessment, specifically in incorporating the "soft" element into the equation. For the personnel to form good judgment on money laundering risk, both internal and external factors play significant roles; and these factors could act as the anchor and supporting factors. No one factor works in isolation, as these factors would interactively influence personnel involved in their task of assessing money laundering risk.

2. Behavioural Decision Theory

Behavioural decision theory (Edwards, 1961) provides a promising explanation for the interaction of internal and external factors that could affect a person's behaviour. Edwards advocates that there are two essential elements in behavioural decision theory which are: (1) the conditional nature of optimal models; and (2) the relationship between task structure, cognitive representations of tasks and human information-processing capabilities. Einhorn and Hogarth (1981), based on extended work on Edwards' theory, has contributed to changing the orientation of individual's judgment and decision-making to look at the cognitive psychology that concentrates on the behavioural aspect of a person in making a decision. Their propositions include both internal factors (personal characteristics) and external factors (environment of the society, professional bodies, or workplace where the individual is being employed) that could influence a person's behaviour.

In essence, behavioural decision theory resembles social cognitive theory (Bandura, 1977, 1986) and attribution theory (Kelley, 1967; Orpen, 1980) as it interrelates the behaviour of an individual in forming judgment posited by those theories. As shown by Figure 1, behavioural-decision theory connects the individual cognitive ability and behaviour as the internal factors while the environmental elements are the external factors. This distinction signifies behavioural decision theory as the prominent theoretical background that supports the manifestation of both internal factors (personal and behavioural factors) and external factors (environment and situation at a workplace where the individual is being employed) that exert considerable influence on individual judgment.

Prior to the development of behavioural decision theory by Edwards (1961), decision-making was customarily shaped by normative models of choices and probabilities. The decision-maker needs to define the problem carefully, gather as much information as possible quite often within a limited time constraint, assess alternative courses of action, consider the consequences of each alternative and make a decision. In actual situations, however, these normative models failed to recognise that decision-maker, recognised by Edwards as "economic man", do not always make optimal use of available information, do not satisfactorily respond to uncertainties and probabilities, and do not always follow the prescribed methods (Edwards, 1954). It was agreed that human beings are neither perfectly consistent nor perfectly sensitive to the information supplied to them in making decisions. Based on the flawed normative models, behavioural decision theory was developed to study how people actually make a decision in broad interdisciplinary fields including accounting and economics.

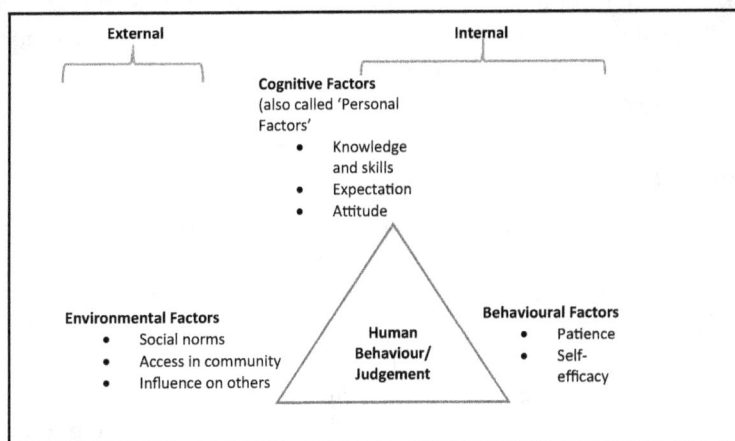

Figure 1. Behavioural Decision Theory
Source: Adapted from Edwards (1954, 1961)

The arguments for behavioural decision theory are often discussed from two perspectives – humans are cognitively limited information processors, and decision-making is context-specific. For the first perspective, people make decisions with a limited information-processing capacity which makes judgment is subject to systematic biases. Human information-processing capability depends on various factors such as redundant and unreliable information, poorly motivated decision-maker and unfamiliarity to deal with a certain task without adequate training. Different decision-maker may process and interpret the information with a certain level of bias based on the ground of what they know about the subject area, not what they know about judgment and decision-making.

The second perspective argues that decision-making is contingent upon the context in which the decision-maker is placed. There is no one suitable model for anyone context as with many decision factors and uncertainties; the decision model can only be unambiguously developed for very simple environments (Joyce & Libby, 1981). Lau and Levy (1998) explore the decision factors such as the complexity of the decision, the expertise of the decision-maker, the amount of time available and nature and structure of the information gathered that variably affect judgment. This is consistent with Einhorn and Hogarth (1981) who have earlier argued that judgment is always affected by both internal factors (personal characteristics) and external factors (environment of the society, professional bodies or workplace where the individual is being employed). The decision-maker and the environment in which the decision is made are inseparable and should be viewed as mutually exclusive.

3. Bonner's Judgment and Decision-Making Framework

On the same conception as behavioural-decision theory, Bonner (1999) established a judgment and decision-making (JDM) framework that exhibits three components affecting a person's behaviour – person, task, and environment. These components are synchronised with behavioural decision theory to represent the internal factors (person as in Bonner's framework) and external factors (task and environment as in Bonner's framework). Bonner's JDM framework was widely used as the guiding principle to frame individual decision-making in the area of auditing, ethical decision-making and fraud-related judgments. Based on this framework, JDM process starts with the basic question of whether there is a need to improve judgment. Once this question is satisfied with a positive answer, then the next big question is what are the variables that affect the judgment – which Bonner classified into person, task, and environment factors.

Past studies on JDM focused on two basic issues which are the quality of judgment and determinants of good and bad judgment (Hammersley, 2011; Wedemeyer, 2010). These two issues are interrelated and should be tackled from the perspective of "problem" and "remedy". Factors that lead to low-quality JDM can be viewed as "problem" while factors that lead to high-quality JDM can be deemed as "remedy" to the "problem" (Bonner, 1999). Bonner (1999) indicated that "problem" and "remedy" of JDM include both input and process factors. Input factors are the factors that a decision-maker brings to the task (such as knowledge) or faces while doing the task (such as time pressure). Process factors, on the other hand, reflect the procedures a decision-maker goes through in the JDM process. For instance, the different search strategies opted by a person looking for information on the internet.

Bonner's JDM framework pays particular attention to task variable, emphasising the need to apply general institutional knowledge and task-specific institutional knowledge in the JDM process. General institutional knowledge typically relates to functional areas within the accounting field such as managerial accounting. Having general institutional knowledge means that the individual performing JDM understands the organisational factors that influence their work, the characteristics that are perceived to be important in their work and the sources of information that they gathered within the institution. On the other hand, task-specific institutional knowledge specifies detailed steps an individual must go through in performing a task and the skills needed to perform those steps adequately. Task-specific institutional knowledge is gained through a process call task analysis, which Bonner recognised can be "painfully detailed" but is absolutely critical for JDM (Bonner, 1999, p. 392). Recognising the importance of JDM, Bonner developed a framework that delineates the logical progression of JDM and incorporates practical concerns for decision-maker, as shown in Figure 2.

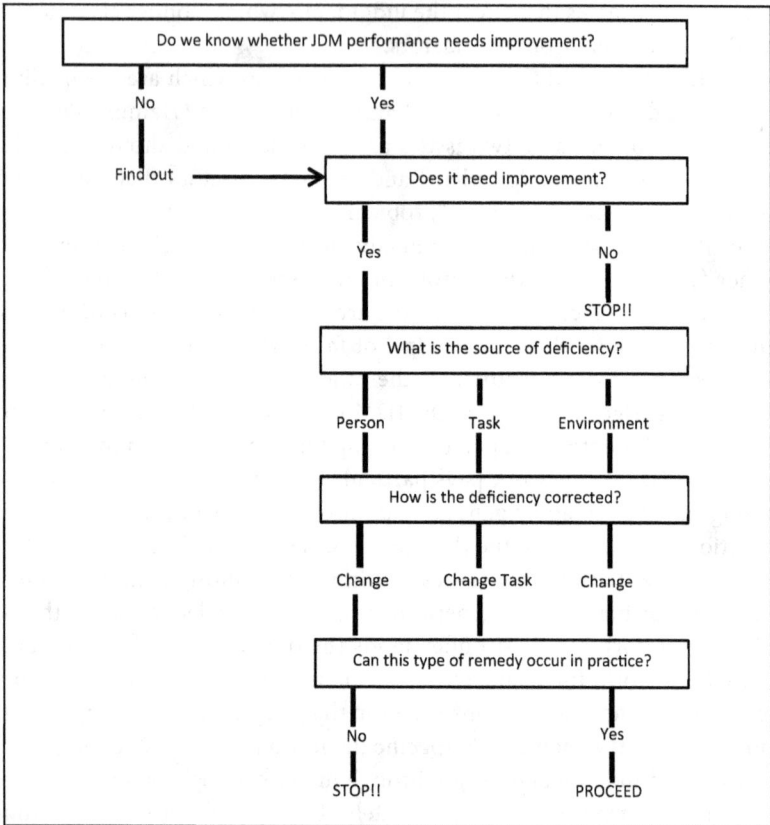

Figure 2. Bonner's JDM Framework
Source: Bonner (1999)

Bonner explains that person variables denote the individual characteristic exhibit while performing the task, for example, knowledge and experience; task variables relate to dimensions of the task, for example, complexity of the task being performed; and environment variables concern with the conditions and circumstances surrounding an individual while performing a JDM task, for example, time pressure. Once the variables that affect JDM have been identified, the next step is to determine how to correct the observed deficiencies for each variable category. For every category, the identified problems with each variable need to be further studied and solutions are proposed. Bonner argued that understanding the factors that affect JDM helps narrow the "remedy" for the "problem". The final question in the framework is exceptionally unique to accounting and social science fields in general. This question considers whether the proposed solutions can be implemented in practice as practical problems occurring in the organisation may not be the same as in theory and not all proposed solutions are suitable in all circumstances. The logical solution to this problem is to reduce time pressure by increasing the time given to a certain task. Nevertheless, this suggestion may not be feasible considering the challenges that the auditing firms face in today's competitive environment to complete the work within the time frame provided.

4. Modified Simon's Model for Money Laundering Risk Assessment

The original Simon's model on decision-making (Simon, 1977) demonstrates that the basic unit of decision is behaviour. This model depicts that behaviour of a person in the decision-making process is substantively rational, given the requirement to achieve certain goals within limits imposed, characterised by the environment in which the decision takes place. Based on the original Simon's model, Gao and Xu (2009) modified the generic model to depict money laundering risk assessment consisting of three decision-making phases – intelligence, design, and choice. This modified Simon's model is redesigned specifically to conceptualise the behavioural aspect involved in money laundering risk assessment.

The original Simon's model showcases Herbert Simon's fundamental work on the decision-making process (Simon, 1977, 1979, 1990). According to Simon, the basic unit of decision is behaviour; and behaviour of a person in the decision-making process is substantively rational, given the requirement to achieve certain goals within limits imposed, characterised by the environment in which the decision takes place. Simon's original model is built upon the theory of bounded rationality – which advocates that "rationality is bounded when it falls short of omniscience" (Simon, 1979, p. 502). In this context, omniscience can be translated as the knowledge and wisdom required by a person to make an informed decision. Without adequate knowledge and wisdom, a decision-maker would face difficulty in arriving at a good decision, let alone a decision that is deemed as "rational". Simon further describes that failure to exercise good omniscience is largely due to failure to know all options available, uncertainty about relevant exogenous events and inability to understand possible consequences.

Gao and Xu (2009) have remodelled Simon's model for generic decision-making to specifically suit the context of money laundering risk assessment. The

modified model is conceptualised to develop an intelligent agent-assisted decision support system for money laundering risk assessment. Despite the intended
purpose of this modified model is for system development, it can be used to
model human decision-making process as it is essentially built based on basic
decision-making principles. Figure 3 exhibits the modified Simon's model for
money laundering risk assessment, which shows the specific activities in each
phase – i.e. intelligence, design and choice that is embodied by the personnel
involved in money laundering risk assessment.

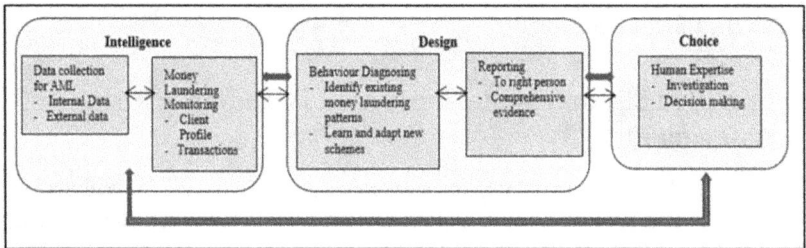

Figure 3. Modified Simon's Model for Money Laundering Risk Assessment
Source: Gao & Xu (2009)

In the intelligence phase, information related to customers is gathered from the
internal and external sources. Internal data can be from the systems that the
affected institutions refer to in screening out the customers' identities, such as
Banker's Equity, World Check and Dow Jones. External data are the data gathered from the customers themselves such as identification documents and evidence on the source of income. These two different sources of data allow for
better analysis of the impending risk given that human possesses the intelligence
to decipher the information. The monitoring of customers' profiles and transactions also requires human involvement. Despite the fact that automated solutions may have the capability of analysing transactions, particularly given the
high volume and complexity of the transactions, human intelligence is a prereq-
uisite in screening out threshold reporting provided by the automated solutions
(Knapp & Knapp, 2001).

    In the design phase, it is first necessary to analyse the data collected from the
intelligence phase. Based on the data gathered, the possibility of money laundering risk is investigated and diagnosed (Gao & Xu, 2009). At this stage, it is
very important to establish suspicious patterns of behaviour that may be hidden
behind client profiles and transactions. It is also important to learn and adapt to

new sophisticated money laundering schemes developed over time. Good understanding of the indicators or red flags of money laundering provides a steep learning curve on the signs of money laundering activities. Human intelligence is still needed in this phase to understand and characterise the patterns and schemes of money laundering which allows for continuous learning on the designs of money laundering activities.

In the choice phase, human expertise and judgment are required in the assessment of money laundering risk. This stage is crucial as the final decision to report a suspicion lies in the judgment of whether there is enough suspicion worthy of reporting and taking action (Gao & Xu, 2009). In this phase, the information gathered may not be adequate to call for a decision; hence, more information would be required before making the final choice. These requests and responses of information are indicated by the bidirectional arrows. The information requesting and providing can occur at all the three phases to and from.

5. Hybrid Model for Money Laundering Risk Assessment

Based on the three theoretical foundations presented above – behavioural decision theory, Bonner's JDM framework and modified Simon's model – a hybrid model is conceptualised to holistically explain the internal and external factors influencing money laundering risk assessment. The integration of the three different theoretical foundations into one hybrid model is empirically supported with a study on money laundering risk assessment, that has shaped the mapping of the relevant variables (Mat Isa, 2019). The hybrid model, which is mapped to the three theoretical foundations, is presented in Figure 4.

There is a duplication for the intelligence phase that acts as both the internal and external factors as a person's intelligence can be sourced internally and externally. Hence, the hybrid model shows that Bonner's JDM framework and Simon's modified model are both accommodating to behavioural decision theory as the main theoretical framework, which shows the mapping of their respective dimension of factors to the internal and external factors in influencing money laundering risk assessment.

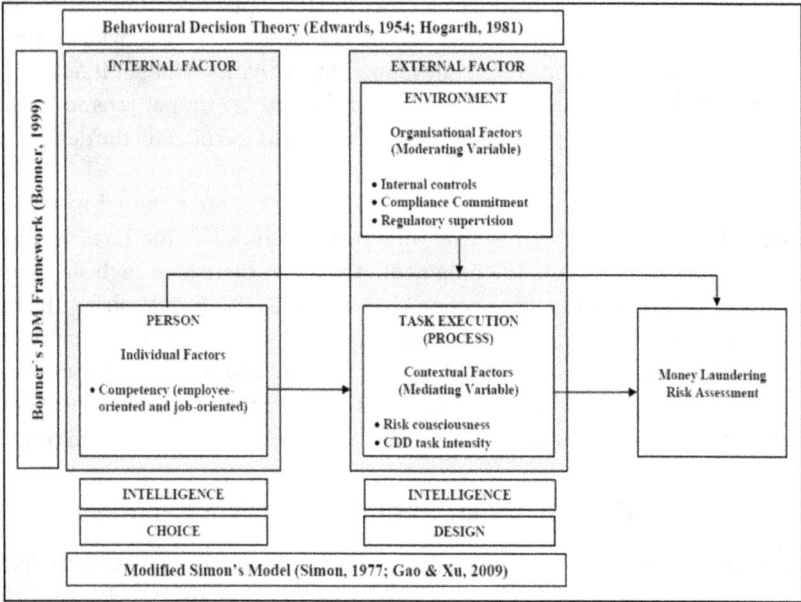

Figure 4. Hybrid Model for Money Laundering Risk Assessment

In the context of money laundering risk assessment, the hybrid model show-cases some examples of variables that are classified as external and internal factors, which are mapped in the dimensions of person, task and environment. The person dimension, which represents the individual factor recognised as the anchor element that could have influenced an individual judgment, is deemed as the intrinsic internal factor within the personnel involved in assessing money laundering risk. This individual factor also represents the intelligence and choice that the personnel could personify. One example of an individual factor is competency that could be categorised into employee-oriented and job-oriented competency.

For the external factor, two dimensions are theorised to influence money laundering risk assessment, that is, task and environment. Task factors are those which relate to the tasks of job being executed by the personnel. Examples of task factors are risk consciousness and customer due diligence (CDD) task intensity. Consciousness against risks is a dominant logic for developing professional judgment (Asare et al., 2009). Consciousness against the risk exposure is built across time based on the personnel experiences. Based on risk exposures, consciousness on money laundering risk provides the personnel with the cues that similar judgment needs to be exercised in the event they are faced with similar circumstances while assessing money laundering risk. CDD task intensity should be appropriate to the customer's profile and proportionate to the level of risk posed by the customers.

The other external factor, which depicts environmental dimension, covers the factors that are peripheral to the individual personnel. It acts as the surrounding dimension influencing the personnel judgment through external forces. Examples of environmental factors are internal controls, compliance commitment and regulatory supervision. Internal controls are the in setting up policies and procedures that provide the personnel with control mechanisms on how to better assess money laundering risk, for instance, the requirement to verify the identity of the customers by validating their identification documents. Compliance commitment is the dedication of the affected institutions in promoting the importance for their operations to comply with applicable laws, regulations and rules prescribed by authorities. Regulatory supervision is the execution of roles by the regulator, such as Central Bank of Malaysia, in ensuring that the affected institutions operate within the ambit of allowable practices.

6. Conclusion

In conclusion, the hybrid model incorporates "soft infrastructure" that could prove to be vital for money laundering risk assessment. The person factor (of the personnel involved in money laundering risk assessment) is the anchor determinant, and acts as a focal point connecting the personnel to the external factors (i.e. task and environment) that frame a solid behavioural model explaining what intrinsically matters in achieving a robust assessment on money laundering risk. This effectively confirms that individual factor is the underlying internal element of a person which is a requisite for judgment to take place. In essence, the individual-based role is distinctly emphasised, as the individual factor acts as the pivotal influence. The other two factors, task and environment, which are treated as mediating and moderating effects, respectively exhibit that the personnel are interactively affected with myriad of factors. The person, task and environmental factors need to co-exist and co-react to improve personnel judgment in assessing money laundering risk. Future research could further explore this hybrid model by testing multiple variables that could affect money laundering risk in the affected institutions.

Acknowledgement

The authors would like to extend their gratitude to the Accounting Research Institute, HiCOE and Universiti Teknologi MARA for funding this research under the TNCPI Grant - Digital Transformation and the Fight Against Money Laundering: Enhancing Compliance Efforts among Financial Institutions, with reference number 600-TNCPI 5/3/DDJ (ARI) (001/2023).

References

Asare, S. K., Cianci, A. M., & Tsakumis, G. T. (2009). The impact of competing goals, experience, and litigation consciousness on auditors' judgments. *International Journal of Auditing, 13*(3), 223–236.

Bandura, A. (1977). *Social learning theory.* Stanford University: General Learning Corporation.

Bandura, A. (1986). *Social foundations of thought and action: A social cognitive theory.* Prentice Hall.

Baran, M., & Kłos, M. (2014). Competency models and the generational diversity of a company workforce. *Economics & Sociology, 7*(2), 209–217.

Bonner, S. E. (1999). Judgement and decision-making research in accounting. *Accounting Horizons, 13*(4), 385–398.

Cocheo, S. (2010). *Finding bad eggs at the right price* (pp. 44–46). Compliance Clinic.

Edwards, W. (1954). The theory of decision making. *Psychological Bulletin, 51*(4), 380–417.

Edwards, W. (1961). Behavioral decision theory. *Annual Review of Psychology, 12*(1), 473–498.

Einhorn, H. J., & Hogarth, R. M. (1981). Behavioral decision theory: Processes of judgement and choice. *Journal of Accounting Research, 19*(1), 1–31.

FATF website. (n.d.). Financial Action Task Force (FATF).

Gao, S., & Xu, D. (2009). Conceptual modeling and development of an intelligent agent-assisted decision support system for anti-money laundering. *Expert Systems with Applications, 36*(2-1), 1493–1504.

Hammersley, J. S. (2011). A review and model of auditor judgments in fraud-related planning tasks. *Auditing, 30*(4), 101–128.

Joyce, E. J., & Libby, R. (1981). Some accounting implicaions of behavioral decision theory: Processes of judgment and choice. *Journal of Accounting Research, 19*(1), 1–31.

Kelley, H. H. (1967). Attribution theory in social psychology. In Orpen, C. (1980), the relationship between expected job performance and causal attributions of past success or failure. *The Journal of Social Psychology, 112*(1), 151–152.

Knapp, C. A., & Knapp, M. C. (2001). The effects of experience and explicit fraud risk assessment in detecting fraud with analytical procedures. *Accounting, Organizations and Society, 26*(1), 25–37.

Lau, R. R., & Levy, J. S. (1998). Contributions of behavioural decision theory to research in political science. *Applied Psychology, 47*(1), 29–44.

Mat-Isa, Y. (2019). *Analysis of individual, contextual and organisational factors on money laundering risk in banking institutions: A behavioural judgement approach* (Unpublished doctoral dissertation), Universiti Teknologi MARA, Malaysia.

Orpen, C. (1980). The relationship between expected job performance and causal attributions of past success or failure. *Journal of Social Psychology, 112*, 151–152.

Pok, W. C., Omar, N., & Sathye, M. (2014). An evaluation of the effectiveness of anti-money laundering and anti-terrorism financing legislation: Perceptions of bank compliance officers in Malaysia. *Australian Accounting Review, 24*(4), 394–401.

Sarigul, H. (2013). Money laundering and abuse of the financial system. *International Journal of Business and Management Studies, 2*(1), 287–301.

Shanmugam, B., Nair, M., & Suganthi, R. (2003). Money laundering in Malaysia. *Journal of Money Laundering Control, 6*(4), 373–378.

Simon, H. A. (1977). *The new science of management decision*. Prentice Hall.

Simon, H. A. (1979). Rational decision making in business organizations. *American Economic Review, 69*(4), 493–513.

Simon, H. A. (1990). Invariants of human behavior. *Annual Review of Psychology, 41*, 1–19.

Simser, J. (2013). Money laundering: Emerging threats and trends. *Journal of Money Laundering Control, 16*(1), 41–54.

Simwayi, M., & Wang, G. (2011). The role of money laundering reporting officers in combating money laundering in Zambia. *Journal of Investment Compliance, 12*(3), 49–55.

Wedemeyer, P. D. (2010). A discussion of auditor judgment as the critical component in audit quality – a practitioner's perspective. *International Journal of Disclosure and Governance, 7*(4), 320–333.

Ainul Huda Jamil, Zuraidah Mohd Sanusi, Yusarina Mat Isa,
& Najihah Marha Yaacob

The Importance of Behavioural Judgment and Decision-Making Towards Anti-Money Laundering Compliance

1. Introduction

Money laundering is a vital attempt for criminals to evade prosecution and disguise the unlawful origin of the illegal money from their criminal activities. Fighting money laundering is critical among financial institutions since it is significant to protect the global economy. The amount of money laundered globally in a year, according to Deloitte's Anti-Money Laundering Preparedness Survey Report 2020, is recorded to be around 2%–5% of global GDP, or between US$800 billion and US$2 trillion (Deloitte, 2020). Malaysia's illicit financial outflow amounted to a whopping US$33.74 billion in 2019 and US$291 billion in 2018 (Global Financial Integrity, 2015, 2021).

AML Compliance in Malaysia started with the establishment of Anti-Money Laundering, Anti-Terrorism Financing and Proceeds of Unlawful Activities Act 2001(AMLA) (Laws of Malaysia, 2001). Ironically, even though money laundering cases in the form of bribery and fraud had long been rooted in the Malaysian fraudulent activities, the establishment of the act merely been used for money laundering cases started from the prosecution of Dr Hamidah in 2003 under the AMLA policy. Dr Hamimah Idruss was sentenced to 38 years in prison and an RM6.39 million fine for prosecuting the first person under the said legislation. Hamimah, 64, a former director of Syarikat Safire Pharmaceuticals (M) Sdn Bhd, was charged with receiving RM41.33 million in illegal gains between June 3 and 10, 2003, under Section 4(1) of the Anti-Money Laundering Act 2001, which carries a maximum penalty of RM5 million or five years in prison, or both (The Star, 2012). She was also charged with ten charges of aiding and abetting her employee Yusaini Wan Abi Sabian, 42, in falsifying ten agreements worth US$1.2 million (RM4.56 million) each under Section 109 of the Penal Code.

In combating money laundering activities, regulatory compliance effectiveness is of utmost importance. Ensuring good regulatory compliance has been the main concern among financial institutions. One of the main components in ensuring good regulatory compliance among financial institutions is submitting quality suspicious transaction reports (STR) (Council of Europe, 2020; Ejanth-kar & Mohanty, 2017). According to Bank Negara Malaysia (BNM), every financial institution must submit the STR to Financial Intelligence and Enforcement Department (FIED) for any suspicious activities or customers. National Risk Assessment Report 2017 by BNM has provided evidence that the quality of STR submission among practitioners has been the main concern by the Bank. Even during the recent NRA presentation in 2021, the FIED department representative had emphasised the same issues on the quality of STR submission during the discussion on the regulatory compliance matters. Believe it or not, it is worthwhile to explore the behavioural aspects among the practitioners at financial institutions to link with the money laundering regulatory compliance.

2. Behavioural Judgment and Decision-Making (JDM) Background

Judgment and Decision-Making (JDM) is regarded as one term in accounting studies as an accepted framework (Ashton, 1974; Ashton & Kramer, 1980; Bonner, 1999; Norman et al., 2010; Reckers & Schultz, 1993; Trotman, 1998). Despite their relational similarity, the words "judgment" and "decision-making" have different definitions in the JDM context. Forming a concept, opinion, or estimate about an entity, an occurrence, a state, or another type of phenomenon is commonly referred to as "judgment" (Bonner, 1999). A person who makes a "judgment" can either evaluate the present situation or make predictions (Solomon & Trotman, 2003). The word "decision-making", on the other hand, refers to making up one's mind about a problem and choosing a course of action based on a collection of "judgments" derived in a specific sense (Bonner, 1999). Nonetheless, in much of the JDM literature, the words "judgment" and "decision-making" are used almost interchangeably, which may lead to confusion between the two levels.

Mosier and Fischer (2010) depict the JDM process as a front-end judgment and back-end judgment process to understand and differentiate these two steps. Figure 1 depicts the components of JDM, with the front-end mechanism forming what is commonly referred to as the decision-making judgment step. The front-end is a cognitive method that involves problem diagnosis, knowledge search, risk assessment, time frame evaluation, scenario analysis, pattern recognition, and model framing, among other things. According to Mosier and Fischer (2010), once a person makes a judgment, that judgment will ultimately lead to a decision.

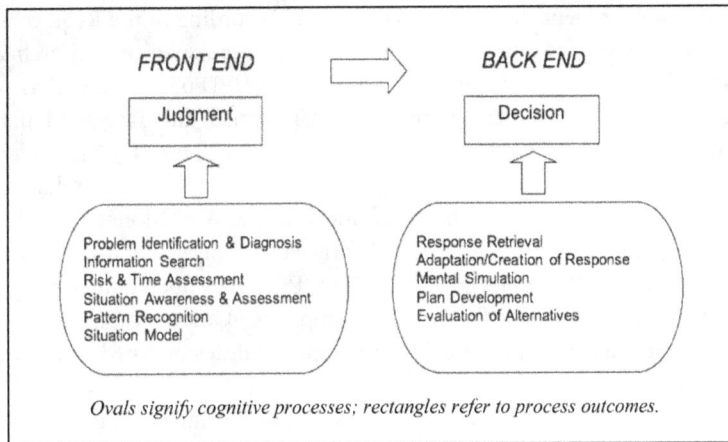

Figure 1. Components of Decision-Making in Human Factors Domains
Source: Mosier & Fischer (2010)

Through experimental study, Mat Isa (2021) investigates the front-end judgment in the money laundering risk area of research. It is worth for future studies to explore the back-end mechanism to the decision-making process and analyse the important components of both judgment and decision-making for the practitioners at financial institutions in conducting the anti-money laundering compliance programme. After discussions about the background of judgment and decision-making, the next section will emphasise the subject matter of AML compliance.

3. Compliance Officer: Why Is Their Judgment and Decision-Making Important?

Compliance Officer is also known as Money Laundering Reporting Officer (MLRO) in many financial institutions worldwide. Quoted by Verhage (2009), these compliance officers, in literature also referred to as "banking detectives" (Kochan, 2006, p. 283), "integrity watch-dogs" (de Bie & Carion, 2001, p. 4), or "financial deputy sheriffs" (Levi, 1997, p. 17), will be the subject of discussion in this chapter.

The Compliance Officer is the person in charge of the financial institutions responsible for managing the risk of the institutions and the key personnel responsible for reporting any suspicious transactions to the Financial Intelligence and Enforcement Department (FIED) at BNM. According to the Requirements for the Money Services Business Compliance Officer issued on 4 March 2016 by Bank Negara Malaysia (Reference No: BNM/RH/PD 031-3) as well as Anti-Money Laundering, Countering Financing of Terrorism and Targeted Financial Sanctions for Financial Institutions (AML/CFT and TFS for FIs) 2019, every licensed financial institution is required to appoint a competent Compliance Officer to ensure its AML compliance in line with the Anti-Money Laundering, Countering Financing of Terrorism and Targeted Financial Sanctions for Financial Institutions (AML/CFT and TFS for FIs). The policy document specifies the requirements to strengthen further the Compliance Officer's capability and effectiveness in carrying out the roles and responsibilities outlined in the policy documents.

BNM expected the appointed Compliance Officer by the financial institutions to be able to demonstrate the following while discharging their duties:

(a) Possess relevant knowledge on requirements under the Anti-Money Laundering, Anti-Terrorism Financing and Proceeds of Unlawful Activities Act 2001 (AMLA) and Anti-Money Laundering, Countering Financing of Terrorism and Targeted Financial Sanctions for Financial Institutions (AML/CFT and TFS for Fis).

(b) Able to apply the AML/CFT requirements and effectively implement appropriate AML/CFT policies and procedures for the licensee's money services business operations, particularly in respect to customer due diligence measures, suspicious transaction reporting as well as risk-based assessment and management of money laundering and terrorism financing (ML/TF) risks; and

(c) Have current knowledge on developments in ML/TF techniques and typologies associated with the money services business industry and the AML/CFT measures undertaken by the industry.

According to the BNM Policy, Anti-Money Laundering, Countering Financing of Terrorism and Targeted Financial Sanctions for Financial Institutions (AML/CFT and TFS for FIs), as per the following section:

11.4.3 The Compliance Officer is required to be "fit and proper" to carry out his AML/CFT responsibilities effectively.

11.4.4 For the purpose of paragraph 11.4.3, "fit and proper" shall include minimum criteria relating to (a) probity, personal integrity and reputation; (b) competency and capability; and (c) financial integrity.

Therefore, as the central role for the STR submission is to report any suspicion in money laundering incidences in their financial institutions, the Compliance Officer's judgment and decision-making are crucial aspects in anti-money laundering compliance matters.

4. Cognitive Factors for Good Judgment and Decision-Making Towards AML Compliance

Bonner (1999) classified three major determinants of JDM: the individual, the contextual, and the environment. The variables or factors that influence JDM efficiency are referred to as determinants. They are intertwined and communicate with one another, and they are essential to the JDM process. Only a few studies have explored the JDM research linking to the money laundering area and emphasised the three components of JDM; individual, contextual and environmental factors (Mat Isa et al., 2021; Mohd Sanusi et al., 2022).

Individual variables identify the characteristics of the decision-maker that can influence task execution, such as competency, knowledge-sharing capacity, experience, information-processing abilities, use of decision aids, and prior beliefs based on previous experiences (Loibl et al., 2020; Mala & Chand, 2015; Pflugrath et al., 2007). Individual variables are the "anchor" determinants of JDM, as they are personal characteristics that shape how an individual behaves while performing assigned roles (Harding & Trotman, 2009). Individual variables are important for compliance officers since they must constantly rely on their personal qualities in exercising sound judgment and decision-making.

Contextual variables define the dimensions of the task handled by the decision-maker, such as task complexity, risk assessment, and format complexity (Ayal et al., 2015; Iskandar, 1996; Lee, 2020; Mala & Chand, 2015; Schwarz et al., 2021). Contextual variables are specific to the task at hand, but they cannot function without the people making the decisions and the environment in which they are made. It is commonly accepted that people are faced with tasks with varying degrees of difficulty (Liao et al., 2011). Tasks that require judgment are often complex, and completing them necessitates significant resources, such as efforts and consistent behaviours (Iskandar & Sanusi, 2011). Compliance officers also face a challenging task in assessing money laundering risk because of the inconsistency of information gathered during the ongoing due diligence, big data of customers, and transactions that need to be analysed and monitored, necessitating careful judgment.

Environment variables refer to the circumstances and conditions surrounding a person when performing a JDM role in an organisation, such as ethical environment, law enforcement, time pressure, accountability, rewards, and internal controls (Mala & Chand, 2015; Trotman et al., 2011). These variables can affect how an individual performs the task at hand and how much experience, effort, and motivation they put into it (Hammersley, 2011; Kang & Park, 2019; Trotman, 2005). The task is for the person to use good judgment in various situations and under a variety of conditions. These variables have little to do with any particular task; rather, they are linked to the circumstances in which individuals are put while exercising judgment, which can vary from one setting to the next (Bonner, 1999; Mala & Chand, 2015). Compliance officers are subject to various organisational considerations in the context of banking institutions because they do not function in isolation and must engage with a variety of stakeholders both within and outside the organisation, such as management and regulators. For instance, a compliance officer who works in a high ethical environment is expected to make sound judgments and decision-making than those who work in a less ethical workplace. Moreover, compliance officers who have always been monitored by the regulatory officers at the Bank Negara, for example, shall be more vigilant in conducting their anti-money laundering compliance task.

With the combination of all three components of individual-contextual-environment factors of JDM functions, it is empirically proven that the three prongs significantly affect people's judgment and decision-making related to money laundering risk (Mat Isa et al., 2021; Mohd Sanusi et al., 2022). More researchers should further explore the money laundering area with the behavioural approach, especially in judgment and decision-making matters.

5. Conclusion

In conclusion, this chapter has shed light on the paramount importance of behavioural judgment and decision-making (JDM) in the realm of Anti-Money Laundering (AML) compliance. By dissecting the individual, contextual, and environmental determinants of JDM, we have gained a comprehensive understanding of the intricate interplay that underpins effective decision-making processes within the AML framework. Recognising the cognitive biases that influence compliance officers' judgment is essential in fortifying their ability to identify and mitigate money laundering risks. Moreover, understanding the contextual factors, including organisational structures and procedural frameworks, is crucial in fostering a compliance culture that nurtures money laundering risk decision-making.

Furthermore, the broader socio-economic and geopolitical environment cannot be overlooked, as it exerts a profound influence on compliance officers' decision-making processes. The impact of regulatory frameworks, technological advancements, and global financial trends requires constant vigilance and adaptability. By embracing an integrated approach that considers these three dimensions, compliance officers can navigate the complex landscape of financial transactions and regulatory protocols with precision and efficacy. This, in turn, not only safeguards the integrity of the financial system but also upholds the broader societal interest in combating financial crime.

In essence, the significance of behavioural JDM in AML compliance cannot be overstated. Through continuous research, education, and practical application, we can further refine and optimise the decision-making processes that are instrumental in the fight against money laundering, ultimately contributing to a more secure and transparent global financial ecosystem.

References

Ayal, S., Rusou, Z., Zakay, D., & Hochman, G. (2015). Determinants of judgment and decision-making quality: The interplay between information processing style and situational factors. *Frontiers in Psychology*, 1088. https://doi.org/10.3389/FPSYG.2015.01088

Bonner, S. E. (1999). Judgement and decision-making research in accounting. *Accounting Horizons*, *13*(4), 385–398. https://doi.org/10.2308/acch.1999.13.4.385

Council of Europe. (2020, September 3–14). *Money laundering and terrorism financing trends in MONEYVAL jurisdictions during the COVID-19 crisis.*

Deloitte. (2020). *Anti-money laundering preparedness survey report 2020.* https://www2.deloitte.com/content/dam/Deloitte/in/Documents/finance/Forensic/in-forensic-AML-Survey-report-2020-noexp.pdf

Ejanthkar, S., & Mohanty, L. (2017). *The growing threat of money laundering to Vietnam.* Capgemini, *7*, 1–24. https://www.capgemini.com/wp-content/uploads/2017/07/The_Growing_Threat_of_Money_Laundering.pdf

Global Financial Integrity. (2015). *Illicit financial flows from developing countries* (Issue December). https://doi.org/10.1787/9789264203501-en

Global Financial Integrity. (2021). *Illicit financial flows in 134 developing countries 2009–2018: Trade-related.*

Hammersley, J. S. (2011). A review and model of auditor judgments in fraud-related planning tasks. *Auditing*, *30*(4), 101–128. https://doi.org/10.2308/ajpt-10145

Iskandar, T. M. (1996). Industry type: A factor in materiality judgements and risk assessments. *Managerial Auditing Journal*, *11*(3), 4–10. https://doi.org/10.1108/02686909610115196

Kang, M., & Park, M. J. (2019). Employees' judgment and decision making in the banking industry: The perspective of heuristics and biases. *International Journal of Bank Marketing, 37*(1), 382–400. https://doi.org/10.1108/IJBM-04-2018-0111

Laws of Malaysia. (2001). *Anti-money laundering, anti-terrorism financing and proceeds of Unlawful Activities Act 2001.* 84. http://www.bnm.gov.my/docume nts/act/en_amlatfa_v3.pdf

Lee, S. H. (2020). Achieving corporate sustainability performance: The influence of corporate ethical value, and leader-member exchange on employee behaviors and organisational performance. *Fashion and Textiles, 7*(1). https://doi.org/10.1186/s40691-020-00213-w

Liao, C., Chuang, S. H., & To, P. L. (2011). How knowledge management mediates the relationship between environment and organisational structure. *Journal of Business Research, 64*(7), 728–736. https://doi.org/10.1016/j.jbus res.2010.08.001

Loibl, K., Leuders, T., & Dörfler, T. (2020). A framework for explaining teachers' diagnostic judgements by cognitive modeling (DiaCoM). *Teaching and Teacher Education, 91.* https://doi.org/10.1016/j.tate.2020.103059

Mala, R., & Chand, P. (2015). Judgment and decision-making research in auditing and accounting: Future research implications of person, task, and environment perspective. *Accounting Perspectives, 14*(1), 1–50. https://doi.org/10.1111/1911-3838.12040

Mat-Isa, Y., Mohd-Sanusi, Z., Sabri, S. S., & Barnes, P. A. (2021). Money laundering risk judgement and decision-making: Influences of customer due diligence process and bank employees' expertise. *International Journal of Economics and Business Research, 22*(1), 1–20. https://doi.org/10.1504/IJEBR.2021.116299

Mohd-Sanusi, Z., Mat-Isa, Y., Ahmad-Bakhtiar, A. H., Mat-Jusoh, Y. H., & Tarjo, T. (2022). Interaction effects of professional commitment, customer risk, independent pressure and money laundering risk judgment among bank analysts. *Journal of Money Laundering Control.* https://doi.org/10.1108/JMLC-05-2021-0046

Mosier, K. L., & Fischer, U. M. (2010). Judgment and decision making by individuals and teams: Issues, models, and applications. *Reviews of Human Factors and Ergonomics, 6*(1), 198–256. https://doi.org/10.1518/155723410X1284934 6788822

Pflugrath, G., Martinov-Bennie, N., & Chen, L. (2007). The impact of codes of ethics and experience on auditor judgments. *Managerial Auditing Journal, 22*(6), 566–589. https://doi.org/10.1108/02686900710759389

Schwarz, N., Jalbert, M., Noah, T., & Zhang, L. (2021). Metacognitive experiences as information: Processing fluency in consumer judgment and decision making. *Consumer Psychology Review, 4*(1), 4–25. https://doi.org/10.1002/arcp.1067

Trotman, K. T. (2005). Discussion of judgment and decision-making research in auditing: A task, person, and interperson interaction perspective. *Auditing: A Journal of Practice & Theory, 24*(Supplement), 41–71.

Trotman, K. T., Tan, H. C., & Ang, N. (2011). Fifty-year overview of judgment and decision-making research in accounting. *Accounting and Finance, 51*(1), 278–360. https://doi.org/10.1111/j.1467-629X.2010.00398.x

Verhage, A. (2009). Compliance and AML in Belgium: A booming sector with growing pains. *Journal of Money Laundering Control, 12*(2), 113–133.

Salwa Zolkaflil, Sharifah Nazatul Faiza Syed Mustapha Nazri,
Normah Omar, Nur Aima Shafie, & Aziatul Waznah Ghazali

An Overview of Trade-Based Money Laundering Risk Indicators

1. Introduction

Borderless trading activities and the surge in internationalisation of organised crime have combined to provide the source, opportunity, and means
for converting illegal proceeds into legitimate funds, or in other words is
money laundering (Moamil, 2014). The Financial Action Task Force (FATF)
has recognised misuse of the trade system as one of the main methods of
money laundering (FATF, 2006). Trade-based money laundering (TBML)
and tax evasion contributed to a nearly $9-trillion loss for developing coun-
tries between 2008 and 2017 (Global Financial Integrity, 2020). The statistic
is based on the aggregate of two methods, which are (i) trade mispricing
based on under-invoicing of exports and over-invoicing imports and (ii) hot
money narrow through unrecorded transfer of proceeds done through informal channels.

According to the GFI's data, more than 50% of the illicit financial flows are
contributed by trade mispricing which is a technique of TBML. These illicit
financial flows have negative implications on country's revenues and reputation. Hence, it is crucial to mitigate money-laundering activities in safeguarding illegal outflows of revenues from the country. In curbing this issue, it is
important to identify and mitigate TBML activities because pervasive misuse
of the trade system results to financial, reputational, and compliance risk to
the financial services companies, banks, and global trade organisations, including importers, exporters, and freight transporters (PWC, 2014).

However, it is difficult to detect TBML because it is done without leaving
any paper trail and the evidence is not as conclusive as other fraudulent activities (Shanmugam et al., 2003). According to FATF, only 10% of international
trade is financed through methods which could be monitored by financial
sector. Eighty percent is financed through banking system, but launderers believe that this method is traceable and have higher potential of getting caught.
Because of that, they choose different method which is untraceable. The re-
maining 10% uses informal financing which involves underground banking

(FATF, 2008). It has been difficult for the law enforcement agencies and prosecutors to detect money laundering activities, what else to gather evidence for court hearings (Mohamed & Ahmad, 2012). Due to this, TBML has become a global issue which requires special attention.

Therefore, this study attempts to discuss on TBML activities, the factors and possible red flags of TBML in identifying TBML activities. As such, this study will contribute to the policymakers, academics and body of knowledge on TBML activities and its red flags among the multinational corporations (MNCs).

2. Literature Review

2.1. Trade-Based Money Laundering (TBML) Overview

TBML was first addressed by FATF (2006) with the introduction of TBML; looking into the definition, TBML techniques and red flags of TBML used by the government agencies in detecting TBML activities and handling TBML risk. TBML has been recognised as the third method of money laundering after utilisation of financial system and physical movement of money (FATF, 2006). Although the methodologies, participants, and situation of TBML may vary, it still involves three stages of money laundering which are placement, layering, and integration. TBML normally occurs at the layering stages (Frangos, 2015). There is also a difference in term of the predicate offence. The predicate offence for TBML is not tax evasion or goods smuggling; it usually involves drug trafficking and drug dealing. On the other hand, the predicate offence of traditional money laundering is tax evasion or goods smuggling.

At the placement stage, rather than using financial system, which is traceable, criminals use indirect activities such as repayment of loans and co-mingling of illicit funds with the criminal proceeds. It may involve cash smuggling and smurfing, which deposits small amounts of money but at different banks, which does not require declaration at the cross border. Therefore, the movement of money is not traceable. As for layering, the proceeds of crime are then designated at different locations to create multiple degrees of separation between criminals and their proceeds. Numerous financial transactions are generated to obfuscate audit trail and conceal the illegal origin. The illicit funds may be layered through purchase of investment instruments such as bonds or insurance policies that will later be sold. The proceeds of sales are then wired through various international accounts. The layered funds are then integrated in order to be used by the criminals at the integration stage. Once the proceeds of crime integrated, criminals may purchase assets, further their activities or complete money laundering cycle and fund the terrorism act (Frangos, 2015).

TBML refers to the process of disguising the proceeds of crime and moving value through trade transactions in an attempt to legitimise their illegal origins (FATF, 2008). TBML techniques range from simple fraud, such as misrepresentation of the price, quantity, or quality of traded goods on an invoice, through to complex networks of trade and financial transactions (FATF, 2006, 2008; Sullivan & Smith, 2012; Thanasegaran & Shanmugam, 2007). Through manipulation of invoices on trade diversion, TBML allows the transfer of considerable amount of money (Frangos, 2015). An example of complex network of trade and financial transactions is black market peso arrangement, which involves drug smuggling, money laundering through financial system and trade-based money laundering (Thanasegaran & Shanmugam, 2007).

The techniques can be divided into two types: trade description fraud and other types of Trade-Based Money Laundering (Sullivan & Smith, 2012). Over- and under-invoicing of goods and services, multiple invoicing of goods and services, under- and over-shipments of goods and services, and falsely described goods and services are classified under trade description fraud. Meanwhile, related party transactions and acquisition and sales of intangibles are categorised under other types of Trade-Based Money Laundering techniques (Sullivan & Smith, 2012). The techniques are summarised in Figure 1.

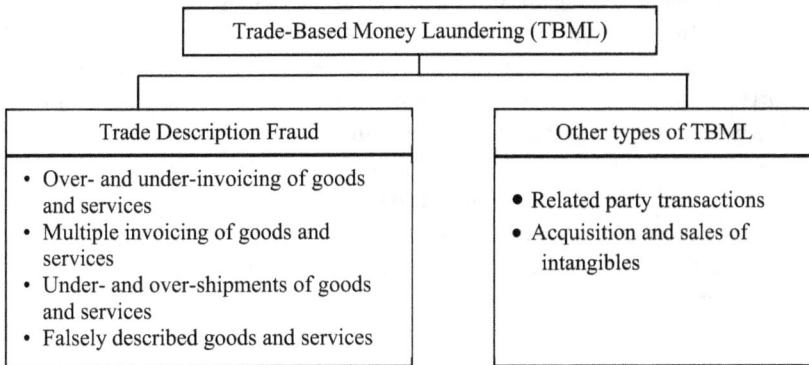

Figure 1. Trade-Based Money Laundering Techniques
Source: Sullivan & Smith (2012)

Trade Description Fraud (TDF) is done through distortion of Inland Revenue or Customs invoices. The main purpose of TDF is to disguise proceeds from illegal activity. Over and under-invoicing of goods and services is the most common method used under TDF and it is done by misrepresenting the price of goods or services (also known as trade mispricing) in order to transfer money between colluding importers and exporters (FATF, 2006; Hollingshead, 2010; Liao & Acharya, 2011; Mevel et al., 2013; Sullivan & Smith, 2012).

Misrepresentation of price of goods or services is the oldest method of fraudulently transferring value across borders in order to transfer additional value between importer and exporter. Under-invoicing of goods or services enables exporters to transfer value to the importer while over-invoicing of goods or services enables exporters to obtain higher payment compared to the amount that importer receive at the open market (APG, 2012; Boyrie et al., 2004; Thanasegaran & Shanmugam, 2007).

Multiple invoicing of goods involves issuing more than one invoice for a trade transaction. Meanwhile, over and under-shipment of goods is done through overstate or understate the quantity of goods being shipped or phantom shipment. It involves collusion between exporter and importer to prepare necessary documents to support the phantom shipment. Falsely described goods refer to misrepresentation of quality or type of goods being shipped. These methods are classified under Trade Description Fraud as they involve misrepresentation of trade description (Sullivan & Smith, 2012).

A newly discovered technique of TBML involves related party transaction and acquisition and sales of intangibles as a medium for TBML (Sullivan & Smith, 2012). TBML requires collusion between traders, both importer and exporter. Since trade mispricing requires collusion between both importer and exporter, related party transactions can make it easier to conduct TBML (APG, 2012). Although there is a higher risk of related party transactions being used for TBML, it does not necessarily illegal.

However, there are multinational companies (MNCs) which use transfer pricing to shift taxable income from jurisdictions with relatively high tax rates to jurisdictions with relatively low tax rates to minimise income tax (Sullivan & Smith, 2012). Therefore, abuse of transfer pricing leads to high possibility on the prevalence of TBML through related party transactions. Therefore, the enforcement agencies in Australia are keeping an eye on related party transactions as it have high risk to be involved in trade-based money laundering (Sullivan & Smith, 2012). This method must also be taken into consideration by the relevant authorities to identify the prevalence of TBML activities. This will help countries from losing their revenue due to illicit financial flows. The consequences of TBML activities will be discussed in the following subsection.

2.2. Risk Indicators of TBML

Common techniques of trade-based money laundering include (1) over- and under-invoicing of goods, (2) multiple invoicing of goods, (3) over- and under-shipment of goods, (4) falsely described goods, and (5) complex trade approaches (Thanasegaran & Shanmugam, 2007). Over- and under-invoicing of goods and services is the most common method used under TBML and it is done by misrepresenting the price of goods or services in order to transfer money between colluding importers and exporters (FATF, 2006; Mevel et al., 2013). The implication is of concern to many countries since it has negative impact on their nation's economic growth. One of the crucial elements in mitigating trade-based money laundering is determining the risk indicators of TBML activities. It has become an issue due to problems associated with data availability and unstandardised measurement used in determining the amount of mispricing.

In response to issues on TBML, prior studies have identified various risk indicators that are routinely used by relevant authorities to identify TBML activities. Customs agencies refer to information written on the bill of lading, invoices and declaration form, together with physical inspection of the goods at the cross border (FATF, 2006). They usually examine the trade description of the commodity and goods to make sure that all transactions make economic sense and are consistent with regular business activities. An appropriate follow-up action should be undertaken when there is discrepancy on the trade and financial transactions. Traders will be asked for further explanation and supporting documents to support the discrepancies (Han & Ireland, 2013).

Other than declaration form and physical inspection, several other factors can also be exploited to facilitate TBML. The involvement of shell or front companies, and third party located at high-risk jurisdictions are also the risk indicators for TBML (APG, 2012; FATF, 2006, 2008; Sullivan & Smith, 2012). This information is obtainable from companies' annual report, specifically on related party transactions in the notes to the account. Involvement of shell or front companies and high-risk jurisdictions is seen as the risk indicator because of its lack of transparency being practised in their jurisdiction. Both shell and front companies can be used to facilitate although it is done in different ways. Shell company has no real operating activities while front company is a business with legitimate operations. Both are used as a cover for money laundering and other criminal activity, and it is legitimised through false invoicing (FATF, 2013; Lo et al., 2010). Therefore, a company which have front or shell subsidiaries in another country, especially at high-risk jurisdiction, is exposed to high possibility of involving in TBML activities.

APG (2012) and Liao and Acharya (2011) indicate that existence of free trade zones (FTZs) or jurisdictions having high import tax/export tax rebates are most likely to be used for TBML. Volume of trade, value of trade, type of commodity or service traded and/or the domestic regulatory environment are the factors which determine the sensitivity of a jurisdiction for TBML (APG, 2012). FATF (2010) defines FTZs as "designated areas within countries that offer a free trade environment with a minimum level of regulation". Lack of transparency and loose policies provide opportunities for unencumbered trade (Liao & Acharya, 2011). Up to 2010, there are 3,000 FTZs in 135 countries; the number is increasing with globalisation of world economy (APG, 2012). Globalisation produces opportunity to illicit financial flows due to TBML. The lack of transparency has allowed companies located in FTZs to create transactions that are untraceable by the law enforcement agencies (APG, 2012; Hoffmann, 2013). Offshore companies and tax haven countries also practice similar regulations. In other words, the characteristics of offshore companies, for example, convenient formation, free operation, tax exemption and financial secrecy, all provide rather good opportunities for tax evasion, capital flight and money laundering (He, 2010). The risk indicators are summarised in Table 1.

Table 1. Summary of TBML Risk Indicators

Study	Research Objective	Risk Indicators
2006 FATF	This study provides a number of case studies that illustrate how the international trade system has been exploited by criminal organisations, current practices of more than thirty countries. This information focuses on the ability of various government agencies to identify suspicious activities related to trade transactions.	• Significant discrepancies on description of goods, commodities • Inconsistent size of shipment • High-risk type of commodity • Commodity inconsistent with business activity • Shipment doesn't have economic sense • Involvement on high-risk jurisdiction • Inconsistent method of payment • Involves shell / front company • Involves cash transaction

Study	Research Objective	Risk Indicators

2008 FATF	This study examines the ability of competent authorities to collect and effectively utilise trade data, domestically and internationally, for the purpose of detecting Trade-Based Money Laundering.	Declaration forms
		• Compare domestic and foreign trade data to detect discrepancies
		  1. Description of goods
		  2. Value of goods
		  3. Route of shipment
		  4. Commodity activity by time period
		  5. Method of payment
		• Cargo movement
		• Tax declaration forms

2011 Sullivan & Smith	This study aims to enhance understanding of TBML, identify the risks of TBML, analysing what strategies and programmes have been devised to tackle TBML and exploring possibilities for combating TBML in Australia.	• High-risk jurisdiction – lax border controls (i.e. Free Trade Zone) • Contra and barter transactions • Shell and front companies • Related party transaction
2014 PWC	This study aims to enhance understanding of TBML, identify the risks of TBML, analysing what strategies and programmes have been devised to tackle TBML and discuss on future actions to undertake this issue.	• Method of payment – extended letter of credit, advance payment for shipment • Corporate structure – front or shell companies, especially those in high-risk jurisdiction • Jurisdiction – high risk and receipt of cash from third party with no apparent connection, free trade zone • Trade goods and documentation – custom declaration form and physical inspection of goods • Barter transaction – goods with goods • Related party transaction

APG (2012) has categorised the patterns and red flags into five categories, namely: Trade Finance, Jurisdictions, Goods, Corporate Structure, and Predicate Offences. Findings also showed that multiple agencies are involved both domestically and internationally in combating TBML, but there is a need to form domestic task-forces. Then, PWC (2014) discussed money laundering risks in the trade finance system, focusing specifically on analysing and monitoring of TBML activities. The report suggested on automated document scanning and aggregation, test analytics, web analytics and web-crawling as means for data collection in collecting evidence of TBML. The report also emphasised on the importance of training for staff and analyst to understand the importance of anti-TBML effort, complexity of the trade system and techniques of TBML. In collecting information related to TBML, there are few documents which investigator can refer to in detecting TBML activities, as outlined in Figure 2.

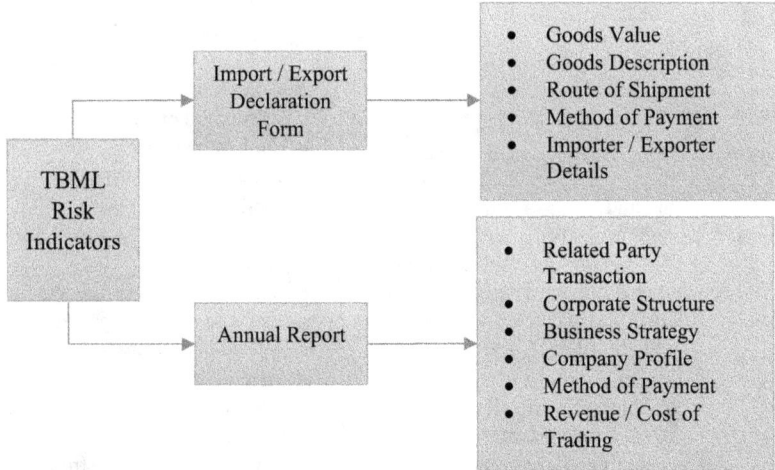

Figure 2. Documents Related to TBML Risk Indicators

Source: Author's consolidation of indicators from various literatures

3. Conclusion

Trade-based money laundering (TBML) refers to the process of disguising the proceeds of crime and moving value using trade transactions in an attempt to legitimise their illegal origins or finance their activities. Lack of a comprehensive system and access to trade data has become the main obstacle for the relevant authorities to detect TBML activities. Therefore, there is a need to have a good cooperation on data sharing among the financial institutions and relevant authorities to facilitate the TBML detection. An integrated database should be established to enable the authorities, both domestic and foreign in deriving relevant information which will help them in detecting and investigating money laundering activities, especially TBML. For the preliminary stage, comparison between details on the forms and companies' annual reports should be done in order to identify the similarities and differences. Differences may result in trade mispricing activities. The differences must then be explained by the respective company and is supported by relevant evidence to ensure its accuracy. The overall overview provided in this chapter is a useful insight to tax and customs authorities in identifying additional indicators that can be referred to in implementing effective policies to detect trade mispricing activities. This chapter calls for increasing awareness among stakeholders especially the regulators, law enforcement agencies and academicians on the need to explore more on TBML and identify possible international TBML activities. Since TBML involves trade activities of two or more countries, there is also a need to strengthen international cooperation among all countries in curbing these activities. There is also a need to conduct risk assessment and risk communication among the agencies, to ensure limited expectation gap between respective parties. Future research may look into TBML risk assessment practiced by respective agencies and propose future recommendation to reduce the expectation gap, so that the initiatives will be able to facilitate TBML investigation in the future.

Acknowledgement

The authors would like to extend their gratitude to the Accounting Research Institute, HiCOE and Universiti Teknologi MARA for funding this research under the Bestari Grant – Islamic Financial Criminology, with reference number 600-RMC/DANA 5/3/BESTARI (TD) (010/2022)

References

APG. (2012). APG typology report on trade based money laundering, (July), 93.

Boyrie, M. E. De, Pak, S. J., & Zdanowicz, J. S. (2004). Money laundering and income tax evasion: The determination of optimal audits and inspections to detect abnormal prices in international trade. *Journal of Financial Crime, 12*(2), 123–130.

FATF. (2006). *Trade based money laundering.*

FATF. (2008). *Best practices on trade based money laundering.*

FATF. (2013). *International standards on combating money laundering and the financing of terrorism & proliferation.* The FATF Recommendations.

Ferwerda, J., Kattenberg, M., Chang, H.-H., Unger, B., Groot, L., & Bikker, J. a. (2013). Gravity models of trade-based money laundering. *Applied Economics, 45*(22), 3170–3182.

Frangos, T. (2015). *Trade based money laundering and terrorist financing: Methodologies for combating the growing economic and cultural threat.*

GFI. (2020). *Trade-related illicit financial flows in 135 developing countries: 2008–2017.*

Han, C.-R., & Ireland, R. (2013). Informal Funds Transfer systems as a target of customs enforcement. *World Customs Journal, 7*(1), 3–11.

Hoffmann, L. (2013). A critical look at the current international response to combat trade-based money laundering: The risk-based customs audit as a solution. *Texas International Law Journal, 48*(2), 325–348.

Hollingshead, A. (2010). *The implied tax revenue loss from trade mispricing.* Global Financial Integrity.

ICFCTF. (2013). Risk, governance & self-regulation "within & beyond." In *International conference on financial crime and terrorism financing.*

Kar, D., & Curcio, K. (2011). Illicit financial flows from developing countries: 2000–2009. *Global Finance Integrity,* (January), 78.

Liao, J., & Acharya, A. (2011). Transshipment and trade-based money laundering. *Journal of Money Laundering Control, 14*(1), 79–92.

Lo, A. W. Y., Wong, R. M. K., & Firth, M. (2010). Tax, financial reporting, and tunneling incentives for income shifting: An empirical analysis of the transfer pricing behavior of Chinese-listed companies. *The Journal of the American Taxation Association, 32*(2), 1–26.

Mevel, S., Ofa, S., & Karingi, S. (2013). Quantifying illicit financial flows from Africa through trade mispricing and assessing their incidence on African economies. *African Economic Conference 2013,* (October), 1–33.

Moamil. (2014). Money laundering and its global modes. A serious challenge to law enforcement agencies. Some observations. *International Journal of Humanities and Social Science Invention, 3*(12), 40–44.

Nur Syuhada Jasni & Haslinda Yusoff

Corporate Environmental Social Governance Challenges and Opportunities

1. Introduction

Today, economic development receives more attention than sustainable development. Therefore, more countries are focusing on growth in Gross Domestic Product (GDP), a quantitative indicator that signals economic progress and profit-making. Consequently, neglecting sustainable development presents an action that disregards future generations. Accordingly, the profit motive affects not only the environment but also social and governance. Many countries are starting to realise they need to generate profit with lesser sustainability impact on the country, which demands a well-planned strategy to balance between economic growth and sustainable development. At a corporate level, Environmental Social and Governance practices are at the minimal level because of several issues: the complexity of management, reactive to constructive, non-core to value-driven, changing consumer demands and data analytical techniques. A sustainable business would likely have to deal with issues of uncertainty, and they could become obstacles or opportunities which depend on the expectations of the company.

Currently, more countries are focusing on Gross Domestic Product (GDP) growth, a quantitative measure that signifies economic development and is also used as a comparison tool between counterparts. Economic development is measured through industrialisation, urbanisation, and globalisation progression. Like a coin that has two sides, for a country, one side is economic development, while the other side is sustainable development. The United Nations has defined sustainable development as a development that meets the needs of the present without compromising the ability of future generations (United Nations, 1987, p. 40). The present trend shows that more countries are focusing too much on economic development and neglecting sustainable development.

During the last decade, the imbalanced relationship between economic development and sustainable development has received much attention. Several aspects of the relationship's interpretation have been questioned as it has significant implications in people's lives. In general, the issues concerning sustainability being discussed are related to environmental, social, and governance implications. Among the three issues, environmental implications are the most talked about, as they involve cases like deforestation and pollution. Another critical problem is carbon dioxide emission due to the burning of fossil fuels, which is linked to terrible human-made disasters such as rising global temperature and climate change (Freeman & Low, 2014; Paetzold, 2011; Traven, 2019; Vassigh, 2018). It is devastating to note that the consequence reported by scientists is that the Earth has recorded a new high temperature for three consecutive years from 2014 to 2016 (Su et al., 2017). Therefore, even though economic development is essential for a country, sustainable development is more crucial, whereby people must not forget that safeguarding the planet for the present and future generations are everyone's responsibility.

An early move in balancing between economic development and sustainable development was made by the United Nations (1987). The organisation had initiated the Brundtland Commission which aimed to attain a sustainable future by harmonising the environmental, social, and economic systems. Although the progress was considered slow, however, over time, more people's awareness of the consequences due to imbalance between the systems increased, and they started making aggressive comments demanding for more serious action. One of them was Sir Nicholas Stern, an economist, who highlighted the impact of climate change on the economic cost and that social damage was the single most significant market malfunction of man recorded; he, therefore, urged rich countries to lead in taking action (Benjamin, 2007).

Consequently, in the Copenhagen Summit 2009, open tensions erupted when China and India blamed developed countries that were ambitious in industrialisation with assertive consumption both in the past and present but have neglected to bear much responsibility. Nevertheless, China and India have also contributed to the increasing level of climate change in the world (Shu & Bazerman, 2011). Furthermore, developed economies blamed emerging nations for burning rainforests caused by unchecked economic greed and population expansion (Shu & Bazerman, 2011). This blame game has dragged on for many years without any significant measures to solve the environmental issues. In Malaysia, a pollution incident, that is, illegal toxic chemical waste dumped into Kim Kim River, made the headlines in mid-2019, which affected thousands of people. A recent study by Statista (2020) indicates an alarming number of polluted rivers across Malaysia which was around ten from 2013 to 2018.

Apart from environmental issues, another sustainable development issue being discussed worldwide is related to the social aspect. Social issues are commonly linked to multinational companies' (MNCs) scandals, which have received considerable critical attention, as their motive seems exploitative rather than contributing to the wealth and health of developing countries. For example, Nike's factories in developing countries faced modern slavery issues in the 1990s, as they were accused of poor employment practices such as slave wages, forced overtime, and child labour (Gray et al., 2014; Paetzold, 2011). Another scandal involved Nestle, which was accused of unethical behaviour due to misleading marketing promotion of milk formulas against breastfeeding in Bangladesh in the 1970s. This case is still reflected among most people today. Meanwhile, a recent scandal, related to Coca-Cola, happened in 2018, whereby this company has been alleged to cause groundwater depletion and pollution in India. Overall, social issues are focused on the human capital of developing countries that have been exhausted (Lee & Kim, 2014) through MNCs' irresponsible corporate behaviours and accordingly, these corporations have received backlash and been boycotted by the public. The Edge Markets (2020) also reported Liberty Shared, the international anti-trafficking group about severe allegations of forced and child labour conditions in local Malaysian plantations and the consequences of banning the import of palm oil products from entering the United States market.

Another major issue concerning sustainable development is connected to governance. The prevailing issue is poor corporate governance (CG) that has led to numerous global corporate scandals (e.g. Díaz Díaz et al., 2017; Skougaard, 2017). One of the most critical events in the 2000s was the Lehman Brothers' case. This case was one of the most significant bankruptcy incidents of all time, greater than the combined effect of General Motors, Washington Mutual, Enron, and Worldcom cases (CBS News, 2012). The investment bank, which seemed to be "big to fail", had been borrowing too much money to fund its mortgage investments and had manipulated balance sheets and financial reports, which accelerated the global financial crisis of 2008/2009 (Stow, 2018). In other cases, poor CG also affected government-sponsored companies. For example, the case of the United States government-sponsored enterprise (GSE), The Federal National Mortgage Association (FNMA) more commonly known as Fannie Mae, which occurred in late 2007. Another example is Malaysia's state-owned investment fund, 1MDB, which came under investigation in 2015. Both these cases involved a major accounting scandal in which large irregularities in financial records were reported.

Environmental and social issues occur because industry players are irresponsible and tend to use cheaper and reckless ways in their business operations. For instance, they were taking easy and irresponsible ways to get rid of chemical waste by dumping it into rivers by using a method that creates undesired environmental issues like pollution. In the social aspect, it mainly concerns large corporations' manipulation of poor citizens by paying below minimum wages and hiring underage labour. Meanwhile, governance issues arise due to unethical CG and lack of enforcement/monitoring by the government. The Global Risks Report of the World Economic Forum (2020) has stated that in the period of 2007–2020, the main risks affecting the world are environmental risks (35.7%), followed by economic risks (24.3%), social risks (14.3%), geopolitical risks (14.3%), and finally, technological risks (11.4%).

Hence, realising that the present concern is on climate change, the United Nations Framework Convention on Climate Change (UNFCCC) has established the Kyoto Protocol with an initial commitment period (2008–2012) and a second commitment period (2013–2020), which involves 37 countries. Meanwhile, in 2015, 195 nations signed the Paris Agreement, which came into effect from 2020 onwards. Both initiatives intend to ensure that all signee nations voluntarily commit to emission reduction targets. Subsequently, to counter the world's sustainability issues, in 2015, the United Nations (UN) announced seventeen global Sustainable Development Goals (SDGs). The SDGs cover a wide range of goals to transform the world, specifically to end poverty, overcome inequality and injustice, and combat climate change. These goals are also working towards Agenda 2030, as 2030 is the deadline for the full implementation of the goals. Aligning with the international agenda, Malaysia is pursuing a few national plans, that is, the eleventh Malaysia Plan (2016–2020) in advocating green growth for sustainability and resilience. In addition, New Economic Model (2011–2020) under the sustainability scope and the Green Technology Master Plan Malaysia (2017–2030) in creating a low-carbon and resource-efficient economy.

A holistic approach to SDGs requires a new way of thinking, as the goals are complex and interconnected involving many stakeholders. SDGs proactively address and solve the challenges as well as create opportunities in four key matters, namely: growth, risk, capital, and purpose (Ernst & Young & EY, 2017). A study by Accenture & United Nations Global Compact (2016), which involved 1,000 CEOs from more than 100 countries, has shown that 87% of CEOs consider that SDGs provide an essential opportunity to rethink approaches to sustainable value creation. Besides, 49% believe that businesses will be the single most important factor in delivering the SDGs and 89% agree that commitment to sustainability is translating it into real impact in their industry. Accordingly, SDGs play an important role in ensuring business operations align with sustainable development. So far, Malaysia has made progress in sustainable development. In 2017, Malaysia's performance based on the SDG Index was ranked 54, with an Index score of 69.7. However, in 2018, Malaysia's performance slightly fell to Rank 55 with an Index score of 70.0, while in 2019, slumped to Rank 68 with an Index score of 69.6. Even though Malaysia's rank dropped, the score for the three years was within the same range. There is a possibility that, concerning the current year, other countries have become more advanced in terms of implementation compared to Malaysia, and, hence, overtook Malaysia's position in the SDG Index. Thus, there is an urgent call to improve and work with strategic sustainability strategies to enhance the scoring and rank performance of Malaysia in the SDG Index. Mainly, the government should provide incentives and enforcement to facilitate good corporate behaviour and for companies to respond positively to corporate citizenship.

2. Corporate ESG: Challenges and Opportunities

Nevertheless, at the company level, corporate citizenship is not a new issue. It has been an unresolved, long-lasting battle since the 1970s, arguing about the company's direction of "profit versus purpose". Most critics have stated that most industry players have applied capitalism, which only focuses on profit motives. Hence, company operations that solely focus on profit have repeatedly been pointed out as one of the factors (Buniamin, 2010) that contributes to damage and destruction, that is, global warming and pollution. To date, there are insufficient sustainability initiatives taken by the companies. Regarding this battle, Peter Drucker, a management theorist, has brought awareness to the primary purpose of the corporation, which is to serve the market and the customer, as written in his book entitled Management: Tasks, Responsibilities, and Practices (Drucker, 1974). Similarly, Paul Polman, the CEO of Unilever, asserts that business direction should align with its purpose, which is to serve society, and therefore, should focus on sustainable growth (Polman, 2014). Thus, profit is just an indicator of business performance for business advantages that could not solve societal demands. Besides, business goals should be beyond maximising shareholders' earnings and be accountable for their wider stakeholders' interests.

It is vital for companies to recognise the real corporate ESG challenges, as the outcomes will assist companies in identifying and choosing the right response to ESG-related strategic challenges (Judge & Douglas, 1998). Nevertheless, the inability to identify them will bring adverse implications for companies, that is, over-consumption of vulnerable resources, increasing rather than dealing with ESG concerns, lack of competitive advantage, diminishing company's reputation and decreasing investors' confidence (Campbell, 2007; Husted & Sousa-Filho, 2017; Paul & Siegel, 2006).

2.1. Management Complexity

The literature also documented an issue, which is management complexity. The complexity dramatically expands when environmental, social, and economic activities are taken into account (triple bottom line), especially in managing supply chains (Mollenkopf et al., 2010). Companies need to understand how to manage corporate ESG effectively (Spence & Perrini, 2014) by synergising ESG in the companies' activities, norms, rules, control, management systems, and other requirements. It is a big challenge, particularly when the company is lacking in terms of internal drivers, such as no support system that can integrate the inter-department functions (Koh et al., 2017; Saravanamuthu, 2004), lack of funding to work effectively (Lee & Rhee, 2007), lack of company support and high-quality human resources (Akadiri & Fadiya, 2013).

2.2. More Proactive Rather Than a Reactive Approach

Another issue found in the literature is a more proactive rather than a reactive approach (Altenburger, 2018; Brammer & Millington, 2008; Dixon-Fowler et al., 2013). This issue is supported by theoretical reasoning grounded in strategic decision-making (Grewatsch & Kleindienst, 2017; Halme & Laurila, 2009) and microeconomics (Husted & De Jesus Salazar, 2006). The reactive approach limits ESG activities to the compliance of present existing laws and regulations and ESG concerns if they arise. On the other hand, the proactive approach moves beyond compliance requirements, which is a strategic way, as ESG concerns and expectations of stakeholders expand their coverage. Besides, a proactive approach in ESG attempts to sharpen a company's capability, hence leading to lower costs and risk (Dixon-Fowler et al., 2013) and a distinct competitive advantage (Brammer & Millington, 2008; Grewatsch & Kleindienst, 2017).

2.3. Moving From Non-Core to Value-Driven in Their Daily Activities

This study also identified the current issue, whereby companies are moving from non-core to value-driven in their daily activities. Consequently, a company with limited resources should focus on areas directly related to the company's core business mission, namely internal operational processes, environmental management practices (Krause et al., 2009) and activities that are pertinent to either the primary or secondary stakeholders' interests (Brammer & Pavelin, 2006). Otherwise, ESG initiatives will not be impactful, as shown by previous studies (Chang et al., 2014; Ting & Yin, 2018). Moreover, many studies found that strategic ESG activities that are focusing on primary stakeholders' interests (suppliers and customers) can influence financial performance positively (Brammer & Pavelin, 2006; Chang et al., 2014; Ting & Yin, 2018).

2.4. Evolving Customer Demands

Next is the evolving customer demands. Lately, the customer evolution is pushing companies to move their focus to product-driven from process-driven initiatives only (Busch & Hoffmann, 2011; Jayachandran et al., 2013; Kurapatskie & Darnall, 2013). Jayachandran et al. (2013) explained that stakeholders have difficulty in evaluating internal process information, and for that reason, companies should understand that it will not work for them. It is not easy to communicate something unrelated to them directly. Thus, companies are shifting to product-driven activities, such as organic, bio-degradable products, which are easy to communicate and appreciated by stakeholders compared to process-driven, that is, the certification process, International Organisation for Standardisation (ISO).

2.5. Data Analytic Strategies

Companies need to collect more data, information and facts as well as adopt an analytic strategy to organise their adaptation towards the shifting setting as well as the advancement of internal procedures (Hart, 1995). The companies must also act responsibly and reconsider the current operation (Epstein, 2008) of all companies within the group. Besides, the companies must also ascertain the best way to become more sustainably efficient (Guillamon-Saorin et al., 2018) and handle uncertainties to accelerate company culture. Nevertheless, there is a discussion that large corporates have internal capabilities that encourage internal and external outcomes. However, medium and small corporates may also increase internal components that keep the internal implementation of ESG (Baumann-Pauly et al., 2013). Companies can have their own strategic planning (Judge & Douglas, 1998) and determine the most effective and best practices that make an interesting starting point (Grewatsch & Kleindienst, 2017).

3. Conclusion

In conclusion, the studies show that management complexity, reactive to proactive, non-core to value-driven, evolving customer demands and data analytic strategies have the possibility to become challenges or opportunities, depending on the company's perceptions. A sustainable company will probably need to deal with uncertainties and issues, and it could become a challenge (wrong sides) or opportunity (right sides), which depends on company perceptions. However, companies will benefit if they successfully overcome the challenges and focus on the possibilities instead. The benefits include critical competitive advantage, cost savings, customer engagement, acquired innovation skills, and handling risk management. When companies acknowledge their social obligation, they gain employees, consumers, and society's confidence in their sustainable business models.

References

Accenture & United Nations Global Compact. (2016). *The UN global compact-accenture Strategy CEO study*.

Akadiri, P. O., & Fadiya, O. O. (2013). Empirical analysis of the determinants of environmentally sustainable practices in the UK construction industry. *Construction Innovation, 13*(4), 352–373. https://doi.org/10.1108/CI-05-2012-0025

Altenburger, R. (2018). *Innovation management and corporate social responsibility*. https://doi.org/10.1007/978-3-319-93629-1

Baumann-Pauly, D., Wickert, C., Spence, L. J., & Scherer, A. G. (2013). Organizing corporate social responsibility in small and large firms: Size matters. *Journal of Business Ethics, 115*(4), 693–705. https://doi.org/10.1007/s10551-013-1827-7

Benjamin, A. (2007). *Stern: Climate change a "market failure"*. Retrieved May 30, 2019, from https://www.theguardian.com/environment/2007/nov/29/climatechange.carbonemissions

Brammer, S. J., & Pavelin, S. (2006). Corporate reputation and social performance: The importance of fit. *Journal of Management Studies, 43*(3), 435–455. https://doi.org/10.1111/j.1467-6486.2006.00597.x

Brammer, S., & Millington, A. (2008). Does it pay to be different? An analysis of the relationship between corporate social and financial performance. *Strategic Management Journal, 29*(12), 1325–1343. https://doi.org/10.1002/smj.714

Buniamin, S. (2010). The quantity and quality of environmental reporting in annual report of public listed companies in Malaysia. *Issues in Social & Environmental Accounting, 4*(2), 115–135. https://doi.org/10.22164/isea.v4i2.50

Busch, T., & Hoffmann, V. H. (2011). How hot is your bottom line? Linking carbon and financial performance. *Business & Society, 50*(2), 233–265. https://doi.org/10.1177/0007650311398780

CBS News. (2012). *The case against Lehman Brothers.* Retrieved July 26, 2020, from https://www.cbsnews.com/news/the-case-against-lehman-broth ers-23-04-2012/

Chang, K., Kim, I., & Li, Y. (2014). The heterogeneous impact of corporate social responsibility activities that target different stakeholders. *Journal of Business Ethics, 125*(2), 211–234. https://doi.org/10.1007/s10551-013-1895-8

Díaz Díaz, B., García Ramos, R., & Baraibar Díez, E. (2017). *Corporate govern-ance in Europe: Has the crisis affected corporate governance policies?* (pp. 73–96). Springer. https://doi.org/10.1007/978-3-319-55206-4_5

Dixon-Fowler, H. R., Slater, D. J., Johnson, J. L., Ellstrand, A. E., & Romi, A. M. (2013). Beyond "does it pay to be green?" A meta-analysis of moderators of the CEP-CFP relationship. *Journal of Business Ethics.* https://doi.org/10.1007/ s10551-012-1268-8

Drucker, P. F. (Peter F.). (1974). *Management: Tasks, responsibilities, practices.* Harper & Row.

Epstein, M. J. (2008). Making sustainability work: Best practices in managing and measuring corporate social, environmental and economic impacts. In *Making sustainability work.* Routledge. https://doi.org/10.4324/9781351280129

Ernst & Young, & EY. (2017). *Why sustainable development goals should be in your business plan.* Retrieved October 5, 2019, from https://www.ey.com/ en_us/assurance/why-sustainable-development-goals-should-be-in-your-business-plan

Freeman, I., & Low, K. C. P. (2014). *Green practices: A comparative study between Southeast Asia and the United States* (pp. 125–144). Springer. https://doi.org/ 10.1007/978-3-319-01532-3_7

Gray, R., Adams, C. A., & Owen, D. (2014). *Accountability, social responsibility and sustainability: Accounting for society and the environment.* Pearson. Retrieved from https://www.researchgate.net/publication/305508510_Ac-countability_Social_Responsibility_and_Sustainability_Accounting_for_ Society_and_the_Environment

Grewatsch, S., & Kleindienst, I. (2017). When does it pay to be good? Modera-tors and mediators in the corporate sustainability–corporate financial perfor-mance relationship: A critical review. *Journal of Business Ethics, 145*, 383–416. https://doi.org/10.1007/s10551-015-2852-5

Guillamon-Saorin, E., Kapelko, M., & Stefanou, S. (2018). Corporate social re-sponsibility and operational inefficiency: A dynamic approach. *Sustainability, 10*(7), 2277. https://doi.org/10.3390/su10072277

Halme, M., & Laurila, J. (2009). Philanthropy, integration or innovation? Exploring the financial and societal outcomes of different types of corporate responsibility. *Journal of Business Ethics*, *84*(3), 325–339. https://doi.org/10.1007/s10551-008-9712-5

Hart, S. L. (1995). A natural-resource-based view of the firm. *Academy of Management Review*, *20*(4), 986–1014. https://doi.org/10.5465/amr.1995.9512280033

Husted, B. W., & De Jesus Salazar, J. (2006). Taking friedman seriously: Maximizing profits and social performance. *Journal of Management Studies*, *43*(1), 75–91. https://doi.org/10.1111/j.1467-6486.2006.00583.x

Jayachandran, S., Kalaignanam, K., & Eilert, M. (2013). Product and environmental social performance: Varying effect on firm performance. *Strategic Management Journal*. Wiley. https://doi.org/10.2307/24037236

Judge, W. Q., & Douglas, T. J. (1998). Performance implications of incorporating natural environmental issues into the strategic planning process: An empirical assessment. *Journal of Management Studies*, *35*(2), 241–262. https://doi.org/10.1111/1467-6486.00092

Koh, S. C. L., Gunasekaran, A., Morris, J., Obayi, R., & Ebrahimi, S. M. (2017). Conceptualizing a circular framework of supply chain resource sustainability. *International Journal of Operations and Production Management*, *37*(10), 1520–1540. https://doi.org/10.1108/IJOPM-02-2016-0078

Krause, D. R., Vachon, S., & Klassen, R. D. (2009). Special topic forum on sustainable supply chain management: Introduction and reflections on the role of purchasing management. *Journal of Supply Chain Management*, *45*(4), 18–25. https://doi.org/10.1111/j.1745-493X.2009.03173.x

Kurapatskie, B., & Darnall, N. (2013). Which corporate sustainability activities are associated with greater financial payoffs? *Business Strategy and the Environment*, *22*(1), 49–61. https://doi.org/10.1002/bse.1735

Lee, K.-H., & Kim, C. H. (2014). *Corporate social responsibility (CSR) practice and implementation within the institutional context: The case of the Republic of Korea* (pp. 65–82). Springer. https://doi.org/10.1007/978-3-319-01532-3_4

Lee, S. Y., & Rhee, S. K. (2007). The change in corporate environmental strategies: A longitudinal empirical study. *Management Decision*, *45*(2), 196–216. https://doi.org/10.1108/00251740710727241

Mollenkopf, D., Stolze, H., Tate, W. L., & Ueltschy, M. (2010). Green, lean, and global supply chains. *International Journal of Physical Distribution and Logistics Management*, *40*(1-2), 14–41. https://doi.org/10.1108/09600031011018028

Paetzold, F. (2011). Sustainable investing in Asia: Uncovering opportunities and risks. In *Responsible management in Asia* (pp. 256–276). Palgrave Macmillan UK. https://doi.org/10.1057/9780230306806_16

Paul, C. J. M., & Siegel, D. S. (2006). Corporate social responsibility and economic performance. *Journal of Productivity Analysis*. Springer. https://doi.org/10.2307/41770248

Polman, P. (2014). *Business, society, and the future of capitalism McKinsey*. Retrieved May 26, 2019, from https://www.mckinsey.com/business-functions/sustainability/our-insights/business-society-and-the-future-of-capitalism

Saravanamuthu, K. (2004, April 1). What is measured counts: Harmonized corporate reporting and sustainable economic development. In *Critical perspectives on accounting*. Academic Press. https://doi.org/10.1016/S1045-2354(03)00063-7

Setó-Pamies, D. (2015). The relationship between women directors and corporate social responsibility. *Corporate Social Responsibility and Environmental Management*, 22(6), 334–345. https://doi.org/10.1002/csr.1349

Shu, L. L., & Bazerman, M. H. (2011). *Cognitive barriers to environmental action: Problems and solutions*. Oxford University Press. https://doi.org/10.1093/oxfordhb/9780199584451.003.0009

Skougaard, M. (2017). *Perspectives on the integration of corporate governance in equity investments: From the periphery to the core, from passive to active* (pp. 33–49). Springer. https://doi.org/10.1007/978-3-319-55206-4_3

Spence, L. J., & Perrini, F. (2014). Practice and politics: Ethics and social responsibility in SMEs in the European Union. *African Journal of Business Ethics*, 4(2), 20–31. https://doi.org/10.15249/4-2-68

Statista. (2020, January 3). *Number of polluted rivers in Malaysia from 2013 to 2018*. Retrieved August 7, 2020, from https://www.statista.com/statistics/947835/malaysia-polluted-rivers-number/

Stow, N. (2018). *Why did Lehman Brothers collapse and what caused the global financial crisis in 2008?* Retrieved July 26, 2020, from https://www.thesun.co.uk/news/7265360/lehman-brothers-bank-collapse-crisis-bankruptcy/

Su, J., Zhang, R., & Wang, H. (2017). Consecutive record-breaking high temperatures marked the handover from hiatus to accelerated warming. *Scientific Reports*, 7(1), 1–9. https://doi.org/10.1038/srep43735

The Edge Markets. (2020, August 7). *Sime Darby Plantation rebuts allegations by Liberty Shared over wage theft, money laundering*. Retrieved August 7, 2020, from https://apps.theedgemarkets.com/article/sime-darby-plantation-rebuts-allegations-liberty-shared-over-wage-theft-money-laundering

Ting, P.-H., & Yin, H. (2018). How do corporate social responsibility activities affect performance? The role of excess control right. *Corporate Social Responsibility and Environmental Management*, 25(6), 1320–1331. ttps://doi.org/10.1002/csr.1641

Traven, L. (2019). Circular economy and the waste management hier-
archy: Friends or foes of sustainable economic growth? A critical appraisal
illustrated by the case of the Republic of Croatia. *Waste Management & Research*, *37*(1), 1–2. https://doi.org/10.1177/0734242X18818985

United Nations. (1987). Report of the world commission on environment and
development. In *General assembly resolution A/RES/42/187*.

Vassigh, S. (2018). *Complexity of sustainable and resilient building design and
urban development* (pp. 65–79). Springer. https://doi.org/10.1007/978-981-
10-3212-7_5

World Economic Forum. (2020). *The Global Risks Report 2020* (15th ed.). Retrieved from http://www3.weforum.org/docs/WEF_Global_Risk_Report_2
020.pdf

Aizad Haroon, Maslinawati Mohamad, Hairul Suhaimi
Nahar, & Nurhidayah Yahya

Occurrences of Occupational Fraud in Financial Institutions

1. Introduction

Internal fraud has been recognised as one of the factors leading to significant banking crises. The fraud triangle elements such as perceived pressure, opportunity and rationalisation may influence perpetrators to commit such occupational fraud. Anti-fraud professionals like the Association of Certified Fraud Examiners (ACFE) and the American Institute of Certified Public Accountants (AICPA) understand how devastating an occupational fraud can negatively impact its victims. Generally, financial institutions are not the only one who benefit from insight into the number of damages that asset misappropriation causes organisations and their stakeholders.

Occupational fraud refers to deception perpetrated by workers against their employers. Every year, businesses in the United States lose billions of dollars due to occupational fraud. In a nutshell, workplace fraud refers to any form of fraud committed by an employee that involves the use of their position or employment as a factor for personal benefit in a way that is an improper use of the company's assets, properties or any other resources. Employers must be aware that employees at all company levels are capable of fraud. Furthermore, a person can commit fraud against their employer without engaging in any other criminal or immoral behaviour outside of work, finding it impossible to spot someone who may engage in workplace fraud before recruiting them.

There are two main methods to get something illegal, that is, by physical power or by cheating trickery. The first criminal type is called robbery, and the second is called deception or fraud (Albrecht et al., 2015). According to the New World Dictionary Webster (1964) defined scams as a generic term and covered all fifteen ways human intelligence can devise which has been done by one person with a deliberate deception to gain an advantage over the other. There can be no implicit rules for evaluating cheating, including surprise, trickery, deception, and other unequal methods. The Oxford English Dictionary (1961) also specifies fraud as a deliberate deception by concealing or manipulating knowledge that damages or benefits other people's financial interests from the perpetrator of the fraud.

A previous study by Kass-Shraibman and Sampath (2011) found that there are many ways fraud can be categorising which are (1) fraud committed between individuals, (2) fraud committed against businesses, (3) fraud committed against government, and (4) fraud committed by businesses. In other words, fraud can be simplified into two categories: institutional misconduct and deception performed on behalf of organisations. First, management representatives' misconduct against organisations is classified as "occupational fraud"; these types of fraud are so common that almost every organisation experiences occupational fraud (Albrecht et al., 2015). Occupational fraud is often referred to as "internal", "insider" or "employee" deception or cheating (ACFE, 2012, 2014, 2016; Holtfreter, 2005a, 2005b, 2008; Murphy & Free, 2016).

Traditional accounting fraud is the deliberate falsification of financial records to gain an unfair advantage, keep a profit, or prevent a loss (Soltani, 2014, p. 259). The American Council on Fraud Prevention described occupational fraud as the "use of one's occupation for personal enrichment through the deliberate misuse or misapplication of the employing organisation's resources or assets". The Association listed this act as wealth misappropriation, corruption, and false financial statements. The reports often attempt to determine the expense, casualties, and perpetrators. Researchers and educational organisations have examined how managers misappropriate an organisation's money for personal financial gain (ACFE, 2014; Holtfreter & Holtfreter, 2004; Mike, 2012). They can be used in various scams, such as the Ponzi Scam, corruption, and wealth misappropriation. (Albrecht et al., 2012; Dellaportas, 2013; Efiong, 2012; Rezaian, 2005; Rothlin & Haghirin, 2013).

2. Categories of Occupational Fraud

In April 2018, ACFE released the 2018 Report to the Nations, which offered a global overview of the costs and impacts of Occupational Fraud (i.e. fraud committed by its managers, directors or workers against the organisation). Based on the report produced by ACFE, they showed red flags. They signed an increase in statistics on occupational fraud cases, based on 2,690 cases identified in 125 countries, demonstrating the tremendous impacts of occupational fraud on organisations worldwide.

In a recent study, ACFE discusses the strategies of perpetrating their schemes by workplace fraudsters. The annual studies have repeatedly shown that there are three broad categories of cases of workplace fraud. They can be known as (1)

Fraudulent Financial Statements, (2) Corruption and (3) Asset Misappropriation. Nonetheless, the most prevalent is asset misappropriation, that is, 80% of cases in the Asia-Pacific region, including the plaintiff organisation's misappropriation of assets. Asset misappropriation is also the least expensive, resulting in a median loss of USD 125,000. On the other end of the spectrum, fraud in the financial statements is carried in both frequency and medium loss. This category represented 13% of the region's cases and had an average loss of USD 700,000. In both ways, bribery or corruption schemes fell in the middle, occurring in 51% of cases, causing an average loss of USD 500,000. Both the frequency and the mean loss of corruption in the Asia-Pacific region were significantly higher than in our global data, highlighting the high-risk corruption present in this region.

3. Who Commits Occupational Fraud?

Among various forms of fraud that companies can face, workplace fraud is perhaps the most critical and widespread threat. Employees are the targets of the first two types of fraud. In the third category, that is, the fraudulent financial statement, when workers commit financial reporting manipulation, such as performance bonuses, or conceal property misappropriation, such acts can also be done by employees on behalf of the company. This would be described more precisely as a corporate crime (Clinard et al., 1994) as the "victims" would become the public and community.

4. What Are the Likely Factors That Lead to Occupational Fraud?

Occupational fraud is complicated to eliminate. Understanding the roots of fraud and taking constructive steps to combat it will help to reduce it (Abdul Rahman & Salim, 2010). According to Napel (2013), fraud has cost the Australian economy A\$5.8 billion. According to surveys, these losses have risen dramatically in challenging economic times. In recent decades, Iran has seen an increase in fraud cases. For example, the New York Times estimated in 2011 that 3,000 billion toman (approximately 2.6 billion USD) was lost to fraud in Iran, making it the country's most significant fraud loss in three decades. In this situation, forgery was used to receive loans from at least seven separate banks (Goldman, 2010).

According to Napel (2013), understanding why people commit fraud is critical to decreasing the number of fraud cases. Detecting fraud, on the other hand, is not an impossible task; it necessitates a thorough comprehension of the nature of fraud, why it occurs, and how it is committed and hidden (Dellaportas, 2013). The Fraud Triangle Theory was developed by Cressey (1950), which describes the three factors encouraging fraudulent activity among men. Cressey has hypothesised that for fraud to occur, each criterion must exist: 1) perceived pressure, 2) perceived opportunity and 3) rationalisation. Later, Wolfe and Hermanson (2004) reformed the original version of the Fraud Triangle Theory into the Fraud Diamond Theory by incorporating new capability elements. Wolfe and Hermanson (2004) argued that pressure, opportunity, rationalisation, and capability are the four main elements of employee fraud. Subsequently, many studies were carried out to test these theories. For example, Steven Dellaportas (2013) found that all the elements of the triangle of scams are attributable to the deceptive atrocity committed by the offenders who responded to the survey. Other factors include failed investment and non-financial motives, including anger at an employer and seeking revenge by extorting the company's money. These motivations are combined with the lack of proper managerial activity, creating fraud incentives. The criminals have rationalised the idea that no one will be harmed and claimed they would pay back the stolen money.

5. Inherent Risk of Financial Institutions

In addition, according to the ACFE survey, the banking and financial services industry had such a severe problem with fraud that the number of crimes committed in this sector was the largest of all industries, representing the inherent risk of financial institutions (ACFE, 2016, 2014, 2012). Risk can be defined in the banking industry as the potential loss that could result from certain events.

Financial risk encompasses credit, market, and operational risks in the financial sector (Ghosh, 2012). Occupational fraud is an example of operational risk (Ghosh, 2012), which is described as "the risk of loss arising from ineffective or failed internal processes, individuals, and systems or external events" (BCBS, 1998). A risk analysis is the first step to be taken to reduce workplace fraud in the financial industry. An efficient system of internal controls, with an outstanding balance of proactive and investigative interventions, will significantly reinforce a company's resistance to workplace fraud. Nevertheless, the threat cannot be eliminated by an internal control process. Still, well-designed and efficient controls can discourage typical scammers by reducing the potential and the expectation of detection (ACFE, 2015).

A significant effort is to indicate the risk of fraud (Omar & Bakar, 2012). Due to the number of unknown factors required to produce such a prediction, it is also challenging. Hardly anyone realises the amount of fraud that goes unreported or unrecorded, and the exact amount of damage could never be measured, even for those frauds that come to the forefront. The limitations indicate that any effort to estimate the worldwide amount of fraud will be unreliable.

Workplace fraud is probably the most serious and typical of the different types of fraud that can affect businesses. In the United States, for instance, between 2008 and 2011, the federal authorities declared 355 commercial banks and 57 thrift institutions insolvent and closed. Those shortcomings would cost the economy as much as $90 billion (Tillman, 2015). AICPA and ACFE have launched a fraud prevention programme in an organisation that consists of four layers, which are (1) an anti-fraud committee, (2) an internal auditor, (3) an audit committee and (4) a Board of Directors. They are all interrelated functions as they will report to the Board of Directors (Omar & Bakar, 2012). Since 1996, ACFE has published the annual report on occupational fraud and abuse in the nation. According to the ACFE (2016) analysis, workplace fraud costs a standard business approximately 5% of annual sales, and the gross damage of the cases measured exceeded $6.3 billion, with an estimated loss of $2.7 million per case. Occupational fraud is so common that it affects almost any company (Albrechtetal, 2015). Therefore, it is essential for organisations to recognise what increases the risk of fraud and what helps to prevent it. Significantly, the ACFE report highlights that the financial and banking services industry worldwide had such a severe fraud issue that the number of crimes in this industry scored highest in all sectors, illustrating the inherent risk in banking institutions (ACFE, 2016, 2014, 2012).

In the banking sector, risk can be considered the potential loss that could arise from certain events. Issues exist due to the ambiguity associated with incidents that may cause a loss of revenue. Financial risk comprises credit, market, and operational risks in the banking sector (Ghosh, 2012). Operational risk is defined as "the risk of loss resulting from inadequate or failed internal process, people and systems or from external events" (BCBS, 1998), and "occupational fraud" is an example of operational risk (Ghosh, 2012).

A risk analysis is the first initiative to be taken to prevent workplace fraud in the financial industry. An adequate system of internal controls with a good balance of preventive and detective initiatives will significantly improve an organisation's vulnerability to workplace fraud. However, the threat cannot be eliminated by an internal control system. Still, well-designed and efficient controls can prevent typical fraudsters by reducing the potential and the likelihood of suspicion (ACFE, 2015).

Perceived opportunity can become one of the roots of the crime that occurs in an organisation. A perpetrator or an individual takes the opportunity to commit fraud due to lack of supervision, weak internal control and monitoring activities.

Substantially, the ACFE report indicates that the banking and financial services sector has such a severe problem with fraud that it ranked first sector in terms of the number of crimes committed, demonstrating the vulnerability inherent in financial institutions (ACFE, 2016, 2014, 2012).

6. Conclusion

In conclusion, occupational fraud in financial institutions presents a pressing and multifaceted challenge that warrants unwavering attention. This covert threat, often originating from within organisations, carries the potential to inflict severe financial harm and disrupt the stability of entire institutions. To effectively address this issue, it is crucial to understand the underlying dynamics, as illuminated by the Fraud Triangle Theory and its evolution into the Fraud Diamond Theory. These frameworks shed light on the psychological and environmental factors driving fraudulent behaviour, emphasising the importance of mitigating perceived pressure, opportunity, rationalisation, and capability.

Furthermore, categorising occupational fraud into Fraudulent Financial Statements, Corruption, and Asset Misappropriation provides valuable insights into these fraudulent activities' nature and financial ramifications. Recognising that financial institutions, given their pivotal role in the broader economy, are particularly vulnerable to this operational risk, they must implement rigorous risk analysis, establish robust internal controls, and empower anti-fraud committees. Ultimately, the path forward lies in proactive prevention, supported by a collective commitment to vigilance and ethical conduct, fortifying financial stability and security while contributing to a culture of integrity and accountability within and beyond financial institutions.

Acknowledgement

The authors would like to extend their gratitude to the Accounting Research Institute, HiCOE and Universiti Teknologi MARA for funding this research under the Bestari Grant – Islamic Financial Criminology, with reference number 600-RMC/DANA 5/3/BESTARI (TD) (010/2022)

References

Albrecht, C., Kranacher, M., & Albrecht, S. (2008). Asset misappropriation research white paper for the institute for fraud prevention (pp. 1–22).

Basel Committee on Banking Supervision (BCBS). (1998). *Operational risk management*. BIS.

Bierstaker, J. L., Brody, R. G., & Pacini, C. (2006). Accountants' perceptions regarding fraud detection and prevention methods. *Managerial Auditing Journal, 21*(5), 520–535.

Bishop, T. J. (2004). Preventing, deterring, and detecting fraud: What works and what doesn't. *Journal of Investment Compliance, 5*(2), 120–127.

Brucker, W. G., & Rebele, J. E. (2010). Fraud at a public authority. *Journal of Accounting Education, 28*(1), 26–37.

Cooper, D. J., Dacin, T., & Palmer, D. (2013). Fraud in accounting, organizations and society: Extending the boundaries of research. *Accounting, Organisations and Society, 38*(6–7), 440–457.

Glodstein, D. (2015). Occupational fraud: Misappropriation of assets by an employee. *Journal of the International Academy for Case Studies, 21*(6), 125–130.

Ghosh, A. (2012). *Managing risks in commercial and retail banking.* John Wiley.

Karim, Z. A., Said, J., & Bakri, H. H. M. (2015). An exploratory study on the possibility of assets misappropriation among royal Malaysian police officials. *Procedia Economics and Finance, 31*(15), 625–631.

Kennedy, J. P. (2018). Asset misappropriation in small businesses. *Journal of Financial Crime, 25*(2), 369–383.

Le, T. T. H., & Tran, M. D. (2018). The effect of internal control on asset misappropriation: The case of Vietnam. *Business and Economic Horizons, 14*(4), 941–953.

Lokanan, M. E. (2015). Challenges to the fraud triangle: Questions on its usefulness. *Accounting Forum, 39*(3), 201–224.

Majid, R. A., Mohamed, N., Haron, R., Omar, N. B., & Jomitin, B. (2014). Misappropriation of assets in local authorities: A challenge to good governance. *Procedia - Social and Behavioral Sciences, 164*(August), 345–350.

Morales, J., Gendron, Y., & Guénin-Paracini, H. (2014). The construction of the risky individual and vigilant organisation: A genealogy of the fraud triangle. *Accounting, Organisations and Society, 39*(3), 170–194.

N'Guilla Sow, A., Basiruddin, R., Abdul Rasid, S. Z., & Husin, M. M. (2018). Understanding fraud in Malaysian SMEs. *Journal of Financial Crime, 25*(3), 870–881.

Nia, E. H., & Said, J. (2015). Assessing fraud risk factors of assets misappropriation: Evidences from Iranian banks. *Procedia Economics and Finance, 31*(15), 919–924.

Omar, N., & Bakar, K. M. A. (2012). Fraud prevention mechanisms of Malaysian government-linked companies: An assessment of existence and effectiveness. *Journal of Modern Accounting and Auditing, 8*(1), 15–31.

Peltier-Rivest, D., & Lanoue, N. (2011). Thieves from within: Occupational fraud in Canada. *Journal of Financial Crime*, *19*(1), 54–64.

Peterson, B. K., & Gibson, T. H. (2003). Student health services: A case of employee fraud. *Journal of Accounting Education*, *21*(1), 61–73.

Rahman, R. A., & Anwar, I. S. K. (2014). Effectiveness of fraud prevention and detection techniques in Malaysian Islamic banks. *Procedia - Social and Behavioral Sciences*, *145*(August 2014), 97–102.

Riahi-Belkaoui, A., & Picur, R. D. (2000). Understanding fraud in the accounting environment. *Managerial Finance*, *26*(11), 33–41.

Said, J., Mohamad, N., & Kazimean, S. (2018). Empirical findings of mitigating asset misappropriation among bank employees: Fraud. *International Journal of Management and Applied Science*, *4*(8), 25–29.

Skilling, J. (1987). Tone at the top: How management can prevent fraud in workplace. *Association of Certified Fraud Examiners*, 1–12.

Suh, J. B., Nicolaides, R., & Trafford, R. (2019). The effects of reducing opportunity and fraud risk factors on the occurrence of occupational fraud in financial institutions. *International Journal of Law, Crime and Justice*, *56*(June 2018), 79–88.

Vidiyanna Rizal Putri, Nor Balkish Zakaria, & Jamaliah Said

Financial and Government Factors Involved in Tax Avoidance: Evidence in Financial Institutions of Indonesia

1. Introduction

The tax collection system in Indonesia is self-assessment. This is one of the causes of tax avoidance. Based on Law No. 6 of 1983 covering General Provisions and Tax Procedures, self-assessment was adopted on January 1, 1984. Law No. 9 of 1994, Law No. 16 of 2000, and, most recently, Law No. 28 of 2007 were all used. In this self-assessment method, the taxpayer determines the amount of tax due, then pays it directly to the registered tax service office and reports it. Because the tax authorities are not directly involved in the taxpayer's income tax computation process, using this self-assessment system permits taxpayers to alter income data and the amount of tax that must be paid. Indonesia's consistent failure to meet its tax revenue goals is largely due to two forms of community resistance to taxation: passive and active resistance. Passive resistance is closely tied to a nation's economic structure, the intellectual and moral development of its citizens, and the technology used for tax collection, serving as a significant barrier to tax collection. Active resistance, on the other hand, involves forceful actions by taxpayers aimed at avoiding taxes, whether through legal, illegal, or tax-saving means. Tax avoidance, a strategy to decrease tax liability while still adhering to tax laws, is a common form of active resistance Another form is tax evasion, an illegal practice of avoiding taxes by employing methods that contravene tax regulations. Tax evasion can also occur when a taxpayer circumvents taxes by not buying items subject to value-added tax or by employing other transaction methods that affect the tax amount due.

2. Background of Study

Tax avoidance is a legal form of tax planning that involves exploiting loopholes in a country's tax law system. It refers to tax planning that is done lawfully and does not violate tax legislation, whereas tax planning refers to a company's efforts to lower its tax burden. The tactics and strategies used to reduce the amount of tax payable take advantage of weaknesses (grey areas) in the laws and tax regulations themselves.

Tax planning is a legal action because the only way to save money on taxes is to take advantage of items that aren't governed by the law. The goal is to reduce the amount of tax paid so that individual and corporate taxes do not exceed the amount that should be paid. Tax planning is the initial step in tax management and is a component of it. Because taxation affects net revenue, the firm attempts to keep tax payments to a minimum.

Tax aggressiveness, also known as tax avoidance. Tax avoidance is a legal kind of tax planning that involves using loopholes in a country's tax law system (Blaufus et al., 2015; Deak, 2004; Gun et al., 2020; McLareen, 2008). Tax avoidance refers to tax planning that is done lawfully and does not violate tax legislation, whereas tax planning refers to a company's efforts to lower its tax burden. The tactics and strategies used to reduce the amount of tax payable make use of weaknesses (grey areas) in the laws and tax regulations themselves (Pamungkas, 2018). Tax planning is a legal action because the only way to save money on taxes is to take advantage of items that aren't governed by the law. The goal is to reduce the amount of tax paid so that individual and corporate taxes do not exceed the amount that should be paid (Natakharisma & Sumadi, 2014).

Tax planning is the initial step in tax management and is a component of it. Because taxation affects net revenue, the firm attempts to keep tax payments to a bare minimum. Tax aggressiveness, often known as tax avoidance or tax evasion, is used to lower taxable profit by planning tax avoidance. Companies that are tax-aggressive make use of loopholes in relevant tax legislation to decrease the amount of tax burden to be paid, so that the amount of tax to be paid is calculated by multiplying taxable income by the applicable tax rate (Frank et all, 2009). Tax avoidance, defined as tax savings resulting from exploiting loopholes in tax legislation, was previously deemed illegal, but it is now regarded permissible. With the goal of lowering your tax burden.

Tax avoidance is not a breach of the law because it is a method for taxpayers to reduce, avoid, or alleviate their tax burden in a way that is permissible under the law (Lim, 2011). Tax avoidance is when a firm pursues a certain tax strategy in the hopes that the tax measures will not be inspected or questioned legally, but it is risky if the tax tactics are found to be illegal (Hite & McGill, 1992). A corporation's owner wishes that the corporation engage aggressively in tax avoidance because of the tax burden (Chen et al., 2010).

Tax avoidance includes three features, according to the Fiscal Affairs Committee of the Organisation for Economic Cooperation and Development

(OECD) (2008): (1) Many regulations disregard the tax aspect, (2) Taking advantage of legal loopholes for personal gain, which regulators do not want, and (3) The tax expert demonstrates tax avoidance and asks the taxpayer to keep it hidden. Tax avoidance is one of twelve various taxation tactics used by organisations or individuals to lower the tax burden payable without breaching existing tax legislation, according to Mardiasmo (2015). And it is obvious that tax avoidance occurs in banks and financial institutions, which are one of each country's main sources of tax revenue (Ebi, 2018; Francis, 2017; Hanlon & Heitzman, 2010; Reiter, 2021). Banks and financial institutions are seen to be able to boost a country's economic operations, resulting in increased tax collections. However, the development of the banking sector and financial institutions is also recognised as an indicator of economic growth, demand for goods and services so that new investment increases, which also has an impact on tax revenues. As a result, it may be inferred that banks and financial institutions contribute to tax income, either directly or indirectly (Ebi, 2018). Tax avoidance is one of the company's strategies for legally decreasing the tax burden by using gaps in tax legislation.

UK Finance reported roughly £27.7 billion in tax revenue contributions from their banking sector, according to statistics from PWC (2019). However, as compared to the prior year, there was a 5.8% decrease. One of the reasons is that tax revenue from corporate income tax and bank levy has decreased. Based on this data, it can be assumed that tax revenue has decreased, which should be based on the year's trend before it rises. According to data from the Ministry of Finance of the Republic of Indonesia, tax revenue in Indonesia has decreased from 2015 to 2019. This is backed up by the significant discrepancy in tax revenue targets for its realisation, which range from 94% to 84%. Companies are said to have engaged in aggressive tax planning, taking advantage of tax loopholes. This strategy reduces the amount of tax owing by utilising Tax Weaknesses (grey area) laws and regulations.

The banking industry handles a large number of financial transactions and corporate activity. This also implies that there would be a plethora of tax income streams available from transactions. Tax evasion in the banking industry is likely to occur as a result of: (i) the banks acting as tax evasion actors through various schemes; and (ii) banks acting as conduits for third parties to engage in tax avoidance.

The government as a policymaker continues to strive to increase public awareness and compliance in paying taxes because many companies avoid tax. One of the government's efforts, especially for the banking industry, was the abolition of Bank Indonesia Regulation Number: 2/19/PBI/2000. This rule relates to banking secrecy, in which banks are required to keep all information relating to customer deposits. This policy is thought to be a barrier to the government getting banking data information. This is an asymmetric information scenario that generates a moral hazard for banking taxpayers to avoid paying their taxes. As a result, the Government Regulation instead of Law (PERPU) Number 1 Year 2017 respecting Access to Financial Information for Tax Purposes was issued in 2017 for tax purposes. Tax authorities now have the authority to pursue tax revenue targets thanks to this PERPU.

Tax avoidance in Indonesia occurs when companies exploit gaps and loopholes in tax regulations to reduce their tax liability. This is often done by including unreasonable expenses in their financial records, thereby inflating costs, minimising profits, or even creating losses. For instance, PT Bank Mandiri was found to have manipulated its financial records by providing excessively high management compensation, allowing the company to reduce its taxable income and pay lower taxes. However, according to (Wijaya, 2017), there was another tax avoidance issue in Indonesia, which occurred at PT. BCA Tbk and resulted in state losses of Rp 375 billion. This issue concerns BCA's objection to the Directorate General of Taxes' tax rectification (DGT). According to BCA, DGT's revision to the Rp 6.78 trillion fiscal profit should be reduced to Rp 5.77 trillion. Because it has concluded asset transfer operations with IBRA, BCA exists (National Bank Restructuring Agency). As a result, BCA claims there is no tax avoidance.

Economist Yusuf Rendy Manilet of the Center of Reform on Economics (CORE) Indonesia noted that there are still various loopholes in the financial business, both domestically and globally. Transfer pricing is one of three tax evasion methods that are regularly utilised. Multinational corporations use transfer pricing to move funds from nations with high tax rates to countries with lower tax rates. Similarly, to what happened in Indonesia, multinational banks often acquired funding from the head office rather than from other parties. Foreign ownership of Indonesian national banks indicates that there is still a transfer pricing gap for banks to fill.

Transfer pricing is one of the common tax avoidance strategies in Indonesia, as evidenced by the cases also involving several insurance companies, including PT Asuransi Jiwa Sinarmas MSIG Tbk and PT Asuransi Allianz Life Indonesia. These companies were found to have shifted profits to subsidiaries in lower tax jurisdictions, resulting in significant revenue losses for the Indonesian government.

Transfer pricing approaches respond to chances for establishing values in ways that improve private advantages while avoiding the payment of public taxes. MNEs frequently shift earnings from high-tax jurisdictions to low-tax jurisdictions (Davies et al., 2018; Huizinga & Laeven, 2008; Trslv et al., 2020). Transfer pricing is intended to analyse and measure a company's performance; but, multinational corporations frequently utilise it to reduce the amount of tax they pay by transferring price engineering between divisions. Furthermore, transfer pricing tries to reduce the amount of taxes and tariffs collected around the world (Harimurti, 2007). Indonesia's tax potential is high due to its large population and vast territory, because the use of this tax loophole results in tax revenues that are still not optimal.

According to a report by https://id.investing.com/ stated, the increasing interest of foreign investors in joining commercial banks in Indonesia, such as PT Bank BTPN Tbk and PT Bank Danamon Tbk, which were acquired by foreign parties. This growing attractiveness of Indonesia's banking sector for foreign investment further emphasises the importance of robust regulatory and tax compliance frameworks.

Apart from that, there are also several examples of tax avoidance that occur in various countries around the world. For example, tax avoidance is estimated to cost EU members 1 trillion euros (Rp. 12,000 trillion) in 2012, especially in the European Union. The British experience has shown that tax avoidance is a well-organised process. HMRC (HM Revenue and Customs) of the United Kingdom investigated the tax reporting of many multinational corporations in late 2012. A case in point occurred with a coffee shop franchisor from the United States (US). The financial accounts of the franchisor, which showed a loss of 112 million pounds from 2008 to 2010, as well as the fact that it did not pay corporate income tax in 2011, were highlighted by the British Parliament. According to investor reports, the franchisor had a 1.2-billion-pound turnover from 2008 to 2010. (IDR 18 trillion). This franchisor approach is characterised by financial statements that are prepared as if the company is losing money in three ways. First, it paid royalties to its Dutch operations for offshore licensing of designs, recipes, and logos. Second, in other nations, paying extremely high interest rates on debt is utilised to expand coffee shops. Third, purchasing raw materials from its Swiss affiliate. However, commodities delivered straight from the manufacturer's nation do not enter Switzerland.

Hanlon and Heitzman (2010) argued that ownership structure is an essential factor that can influence corporate tax avoidance, and therefore requires further research from this perspective. Executives in a company are those who are at the top level of management (top management). Top management, which consists of commissaries, managing directors and directors, is the party with the authority to make decisions. Avoidance of paying taxes by reducing the amount of the tax burden is usually done not by chance. In addition, the executive is directly involved in tax decision-making. All decisions made within the corporation, including corporate tax evasion decisions, are influenced by the company leadership, either directly or indirectly (Hanafi & Harto, 2014). Executive incentives are the actions of executives who transfer corporate assets and profits for their own gain, primarily in the form of high executive compensation expenses, which benefit both the executive and the firm by lowering the tax burden. The size of a company might have an impact on taxes. Companies with substantial total assets are more capable and stable in creating profits than those with little total assets. According to Dyreng et al. (2007), firm size and growth play a role in tax management. Smaller businesses with significant growth rates have higher tax rates, according to the researchers. As a result, corporations with significant and predictable profits are more likely to engage in tax avoidance.

2.1. Underpinning Theory

2.1.1. Stakeholder Theory

According to stakeholder theory, a firm cannot operate solely for its own profit; it must also benefit all of its stakeholders (Freeman & Mc Vea 2001). Shareholders, management, employees, consumers, creditors, investors, regulators, and the government are all stakeholders in financial institutions. Who has a connection to the company and is interested in it. Essentially, stakeholders have control over or influence over the company's use of economic resources.

The company's aim is to balance the interests of all of its stakeholders in order to stay afloat and compete. This is in line with the application of stakeholder theory. Superior technology is required for businesses to compete and maximise revenues for the benefit of all stakeholders, just as it is in the current day. One of the stakeholders is the government. In particular, in terms of taxation. When a firm follows through on its tax commitments, the country benefits greatly. As a result, as a stakeholder, you may assist the state government in getting tax revenues to fund growth (Donaldson & Preston, 1995).

2.1.2. Positive Accounting Theory

The Positive accounting theory explores the factors that influence management attitudes towards accounting standards that tend to influence corporate lobbying against accounting standards. There are three positive accounting theory hypotheses: the bonus plan hypothesis, the debt covenant hypothesis, and the political cost hypothesis (Watts & Zimmerman, 1986). Companies have the freedom to choose one alternative accounting policy to minimise costs and maximise firm value. With this freedom, managers tend to take opportunistic actions that are profitable and maximise company satisfaction (Scott, 2014).

2.1.3. Agency Theory

Agency theory is a contract given by the principal to delegate authority to another person (agent) in terms of the company's strategic decisions (Jensen & Meckling, 1976). In a firm, the separation of ownership by the Principal and control by the Agent tends to cause agency issues between the two. The principal, as the owner of capital, wants to see the value of the business's shares rise as a result of his investment, but the management that the principal has entrusted with running the company wants to be paid well. Because of the disparity in the goals of gaining welfare, management makes decisions that are not in the best interests of shareholders.

The basic reason for corporate tax avoidance is alleged to be agency theory. This contributes to the development of knowledge related to tax avoidance practices in Indonesia and the current implementation of corporate governance. It also shows how the government, as a policymaker, can anticipate taxpayer behaviour that can affect state revenues from the sector. tax. Income tax is one of the state's biggest revenue sources. When it comes to paying taxes, taxpayers typically aim to reduce their tax burden; this effort is referred to as tax planning. In general, there are two types of factors that influence tax evasion in Indonesian financial institutions: financial factors and governance issues. The financial factors are debt shifting, derivative transactions and transfer pricing and governance factors are foreign ownership, executive incentives and corporate social responsibility.

3. Literature Review

Debt shifting is defined as interest income obtained in low-tax countries and withheld in high-tax countries in order to save taxes resulting from deductions in high-tax countries in excess of the appropriate tax payments in low-tax countries (De Mooij, 2011). This is most common in multinational corporations, when the leverage ratio is found to be more tax sensitive due to changes in international debt. The corporate debt policy of a country appears to be influenced by local taxation. Multinational corporations frequently avoid paying high taxes by transferring debt to countries with high tax rates. Profit margins and tax liabilities are reduced as a result. Multinational firms, for example, move Intellectual Property to subsidiaries in low-tax jurisdictions in order to shift income and hence pay fewer taxes (Gravelle, 2013).

Financial derivatives are tools used by companies to reduce cash flow fluctuations and income fluctuations caused by market risk factors, such as interest rate fluctuations, foreign currency exchange rate fluctuations, commodity price fluctuations, and other risk factors. According to Barton (2001), Pincus and Rajgopal (2002), Huang et al. (2009), and Oktavia et al. (2019), financial derivatives can be used to reduce the volatility of company profits. This is because financial derivatives have a direct impact on the company's cash flow, which will ultimately affect the company's profit.

Derivatives are also utilised as a tax avoidance technique in addition to being used as an earnings management tool. According to Donohoe (2015) financial derivatives are a complicated type of tax avoidance. Company may take advantage of anomalies in tax legislation due to the intricacy of such derivative arrangements. The cash effective tax rate (Cash ETR) is negatively related with the fair value of hedging derivative assets, according to several previous research (Devi, 2018). Furthermore, the fair value of non-hedging derivative assets is positively connected with Cash ETR (liabilities). This suggests that the corporation held off on realising profits while increasing the realisation of non-hedging derivatives losses in order to save money on taxes.

Devi and Efendi's (2018) research delved into the utilisation of financial derivatives concerning corporate tax aggressiveness in the Indonesian context. Their study seeks to gain insights into the ways in which Indonesian businesses integrate financial derivatives and whether this integration corresponds with tax avoidance tactics. The research explores the interplay between the use of financial derivatives and strategies for corporate tax planning, focusing on the distinctive landscape of Indonesian corporate taxation.

Transfer pricing is a mechanism for allocating expenses and revenues among divisions, subsidiaries, and joint ventures within a group of connected firms, according to classic accounting literature (Sikka & Willmot, 2010). Transfer pricing approaches respond to chances for establishing values in ways that improve private advantages while avoiding the payment of public taxes. MNEs frequently shift earnings from high-tax jurisdictions to low-tax jurisdictions (Davies et al., 2018; Huizinga & Laeven, 2008; Trslv et al., 2020). Transfer pricing is intended to analyse and measure a company's performance; but multinational corporations frequently utilise it to reduce the amount of tax they pay by transferring price engineering between divisions. Furthermore, transfer pricing tries to reduce the amount of taxes and tariffs collected around the world (Harimurti, 2007). Supriyanto et al. (2022) conducted research to investigate the factors influencing transfer pricing and tax avoidance in forty-one Indonesian conventional banks that registered with the Financial Services Authority during the period from 2017 to 2021. The research findings indicated that transfer pricing had a negative effect on tax avoidance.

Companies in Asia, especially Indonesia, have a concentrated ownership structure, which has the potential to allow controlling shareholders to become more active in company management. In Indonesia, the ownership structure is concentrated among a few owners, resulting in agency conflicts between majority and minority shareholders (Hartati et al., 2014). The dominant shareholder, often known as the controlling shareholder, has the capacity to sway management to make choices that benefit only them and are detrimental to smaller shareholders. Management is encouraged to undertake tunnelling that is harmful to minority shareholders by a concentrated ownership structure (Hartati et al., 2014).

Pratama (2020) also found the interaction of corporate governance, foreign operations, and transfer pricing practices within Indonesian manufacturing companies. The research object is to investigate the complex dynamics of transfer pricing in the context of corporate governance and foreign operations, specifically within Indonesian manufacturing firms. This study sheds light on the unique conditions of the Indonesian business environment and how they affect the practice of transfer pricing in multinational corporations operating in the country.

Executive incentives are a bonus given to a manager or other executive who has had a role in a corporation to take action based on the power given by the employer. These incentives can take the form of an annual bonus or the opportunity for the company's owner to purchase shares at a specific price (long-term dividends). According to Sarwoto (2000), rewards can be both tangible and nonmaterial. Both the principal and the agent have interests and seek to attain their respective goals, according to agency theory and positive accounting theory. As a result, executive incentives are intended to solve the problem of unequal information agency (information asymmetry) and conflict of interest (conflict of interest).

CSR (Corporate Social Responsibility) is a business commitment to act ethically, contribute to economic success, and improve employee and societal quality of life (Sari & Tjen, 2017). CSR, according to Andre and Baker (2020), refers to how firms conduct their activities in order to have a positive impact on society as a whole. CSR is a sort of corporate responsibility that encompasses all stakeholders. Taxation is a form of corporate social responsibility to stakeholders that is administered by the government. Companies that engage in tax evasion are not considered socially responsible (Lanis & Richardson, 2012). According to Lanis and Richardson (2012), the quantity of business tax avoidance is negatively connected with corporate CSR disclosure. Meanwhile, Caroll and Joulfain (2005), Preuss (2010), and Sikka (2010) claim that certain companies with high CSR engage in extensive tax avoidance. Lanis and Richardson (2012) found that the level of corporate CSR disclosure is negatively correlated with the amount of corporate tax avoidance. Meanwhile, Caroll and Joulfain (2005), Preuss (2010), and Sikka (2010) claim that certain companies with high CSR engage in extensive tax avoidance.

4. Conclusion

The chapter concludes that tax avoidance remains a significant issue in Indonesia, contributing to the country's failure to meet its tax revenue targets. This chapter identifies two forms of community resistance to taxation, passive and active, with active resistance including tax avoidance strategies such as transfer pricing. The article also highlights the role of multinational corporations in tax avoidance, often shifting earnings from high-tax jurisdictions to low-tax jurisdictions and also points out the role of top management in tax decision-making, suggesting that tax avoidance is often a deliberate strategy influenced by executive incentives. The chapter suggests that the ownership structure of a company can influence corporate tax avoidance, with top management playing a crucial role. Therefore, further research is needed from this perspective to understand and overcome the problem of tax avoidance in other emerging countries.

Acknowledgement

The authors would like to extend their gratitude to the Accounting Research Institute, HiCOE and Universiti Teknologi MARA for funding this research under the Bestari Grant – Islamic Financial Criminology, with reference number 600-RMC/DANA 5/3/BESTARI (TD) (010/2022)

References

Andrew, J., & Baker, M. (2020). Corporate social responsibility reporting: the last 40 years and a path to sharing future insights. *Abacus, 56*(1), 35–65.

Bank Indonesia. (2000). Regulation Number: 2/19/PBI/2000. Bank Indonesia. Retrieved from https://www.bi.go.id/

Hanlon, M., & Heitzman, S. (2010). A review of tax research. *Journal of Accounting and Economics, 50*(2–3), 127–178.

Carroll, C., & Joulfain, D. (2005). Taxes and corporate social responsibility. *Business and Society Review, 110*(1), 73–92

Ebi, Y. (2018). Tax avoidance, corporate governance and corporate social responsibility: The Indonesian case. *Journal of Legal, Ethical and Regulatory Issues, 21*(1), 1–13.

Davies, R. B., Martin, J. S., & Parenti, M. (2018). Market access, regional price level, and poverty reduction in Brazil. *The Economic Journal, 128*(608), 1239–1269.

Devi, B., & Efendi, S. (2018). Financial derivatives in corporate tax aggressiveness. *The Indonesian Journal of Accounting Research, 21*(2).

Francis, J. (2017). Tax avoidance and evasion: Causal factors and control strategies. *International Journal of Economics, Commerce and Management, 5*(6), 30–40.

Government of Indonesia. (2017). Government Regulation instead of Law (PE. RPU) Number 1 Year 2017. Government of Indonesia. Retrieved from https://www.pajak.go.id/

Harimurti, W. (2007). Transfer pricing system and its potential impact on global income shifting and taxation. *Bulletin for International Taxation, 61*(9), 404–413.

Huizinga, H., & Laeven, L. (2008). *Accounting discretion of banks during a financial crisis* (European Central Bank Working Paper Series, No. 979).

Lanis, R., & Richardson, G. (2012). The effect of corporate tax avoidance on the level and composition of CEO compensation. *Journal of American Taxation Association, 34*(1), 1–29

Mardiasmo, M. B. A. (2015). Perpajakan –New edition. Publisher Andi Indonesia.

Ministry of Finance of the Republic of Indonesia. (2019). *Tax revenue report.* Ministry of Finance of the Republic of Indonesia. Retrieved from https://www.kemenkeu.go.id/

Reiter, S. A. (2021). The ethics of tax avoidance. *Business & Society, 60*(1), 3–34.

Sari, D., & Tjen, C. (2017). Corporate social responsibility disclosure, environmental performance, and tax aggressiveness. *International Research Journal of Business Studies*, *9*(2).

Preuss, L. (2010). Corporate social responsibility and tax avoidance: A meta-analysis. *Critical Perspectives on International Business*, *6*(2/3), 161–178.

Putri, V. R., Zakaria, N. B., Said, J., Azis, M. A. A., & Putra, M. R. A. (2023). Management incentives and foreign ownership effect on tax avoidance with the presence of credit risk. *Asia-Pacific Management Accounting Journal*, *18*(2), 311–337.

PWC. (2019). *Total tax contribution of UK financial services*. Retrieved from https://www.pwc.co.uk/industries/financial-services/insights/total-tax-contribution-of-uk-financial services.htm

Sikka, P. (2010). Smoke and mirrors: Corporate social responsibility and tax avoidance. *Accounting Forum*, *34*(3–4), 153–168.

Supriyanto, Q. M., Pratama, B. C., Hariyanto, E., & Kusbandiyah, A. (2022). Tax avoidance in Indonesian banking: The role of transfer pricing and corporate ownership. *Journal of Finance and Business Digital*, *1*(4), 251–270.

Trslv, J., Elschner, C., Alstadsæter, A., & Johannesen, N. (2020). The rise of phantom investments. *International Tax and Public Finance*, *27*, 772–800.

Wijaya, I. (2017). Tax avoidance issue in Indonesia. *Journal of Indonesian Economy and Business*, *32*(1), 1–16.

Erlane K. Ghani, Azleen Ilias, & Kamaruzzaman Muhammad

Risk Management in Procurement in the Public Sector: A Research Opportunity

1. Introduction

Risk is an inherent component of any business venture and has emerged as a significant worry for stakeholders. The notion of risk is often linked to the likelihood of unfavourable events or transactions taking place during a certain period, resulting in adverse consequences for the achievement of objectives. This idea pertains to the potentiality of encountering an adverse consequence due to a certain occurrence. All companies would encounter a variety of hazards while enhancing their internal strategies and grappling with external challenges. In order to effectively contend for resources and establish a worldwide market presence, organisations must possess a sustainable competitive edge and maintain an ongoing need for innovation (Oliva, 2016).

The rapid pace of innovation and dynamic shifts in the global business landscape have presented significant possibilities for the corporation. Therefore, it is essential to adequately and promptly report hazards. Companies safeguard and generate value for their stakeholders through the identification of potential risks and opportunities. The identification and assessment of risks faced by an organisation, as well as the establishment of an appropriate risk tolerance level, pose significant challenges for management. These challenges are crucial in order to enhance value creation and mitigate the potential negative impacts of complex risks (Albasu & Nyameh, 2017; Beasley et al., 2017).

According to Hatvani (2015), the word "risk" encompasses both positive and negative implications of uncertainty in relation to fulfilling an organisation's requirements. According to the Financial Services Authority, a corporation is exposed to eight distinct categories of risks, including credit risk, market risk, liquidity risk, operational risk, compliance risk, legal risk, reputation risk, and strategic risk. Risk is inherently interconnected with uncertainty. Uncertain factors are more likely to engender dangers. Hence, effective risk management is crucial in order to achieve the desired outcomes. In order to ensure the achievement of an organisation's goals and objectives, it is essential for the organisation's leadership to possess the necessary skills and capabilities to successfully manage any associated risks (Pawi et al., 2012). This viewpoint posits that the incorporation of risk management as a procedural framework may contribute to the enhancement of an organisation's decision-making process, hence accentuating its progress, especially within the realm of public sector operations.

2. Risk in Public Sector

The issue of risk management in the public sector has been a matter of continuous discourse due to the persistent exposure of these organisations to a range of dangers that possess the capacity to impact their operations and standing. The need for risk management has notably increased during the global financial crisis that transpired from 2007 to 2009 (Reserve Bank of Australia, 2023). A commonly held perspective among risk managers is that the financial crisis might be related to a perceived inadequacy in the implementation of risk management strategies. Many firms have enhanced their essential strategic risk data and given more importance to risk management efforts (Lalonde & Boiral, 2012). The risks stated above may be classified into several sectors, such as financial, regulatory, technological, and political.

To effectively assess these risks and execute suitable measures to minimise their consequences, it is essential for public sector organisations to possess a thorough risk management strategy. Hence, risk management plays a crucial role within the corporate governance structure of public sector organisations. The responsibilities include the creation of tangible structures and the establishment of protocols that promote success in both strategic and operational realms (Marrofi et al., 2017). Risk management plays a crucial role in enabling public sector firms to effectively adapt to changes and make well-informed decisions. Consequently, this facilitates improved operational efficacy for public sector entities, leading to enhanced outcomes for people and heightened internal efficiency.

The ever-changing nature of the public sector presents challenges for public sector organisations in efficiently and cost-effectively addressing risk mitigation. Public sector organisations encounter several challenges when attempting to establish and execute a proficient risk management strategy, as is also mentioned in private institutions (Chakabva et al., 2021). One key concern is the lack of integration. The integration of risk management is essential to the overall strategy framework of any given organisation. It is important to instil a comprehensive understanding of risk awareness across all departments in order to augment their decision-making capabilities. Many firms encounter challenges while endeavouring to integrate risk management practices into their operating processes at the departmental level. Nevertheless, it is observed that the risk management team often functions in a state of isolation, leading to inadequate exchange of information and a lack of responsibility among its members.

The primary issue is that the absence of employee comprehension of the objectives and significance of risk management might also give rise to difficulties. There are those who may see it just as a routine task, neglecting to fully comprehend its significance to the company and its potential to contribute to overall success (Corvellec, 2009). Consequently, personnel persist in using outdated methodologies that are inadequate for meeting contemporary demands for reducing interruptions. However, it is important for firms to have the support and commitment of their workers from the outset of the adoption of risk management. This may be achieved by providing assistance to individuals in adopting emerging technologies such as data analytics that can assist in assessing risks.

3. Risk Management

Risk management is a comprehensive approach that involves the methodical implementation of management policies, processes, and procedures to effectively identify, analyse, evaluate, treat, monitor, and communicate risks (Gajewska & Ropel, 2011). Risk management is a well-established concept in the academic literature. Risk management is further characterised as a collection of methodologies devised to mitigate the impacts stemming from risks and uncertainties while simultaneously streamlining the process of decision-making. This approach facilitates the identification of significant hazards inside an organisation, conducts a thorough study of these risks, and implements appropriate measures to effectively monitor and manage the identified risks. The primary objective of risk management is to identify the origins of potential risks and uncertainties, evaluate their potential consequences, and devise suitable strategies for their mitigation. The primary obstacle faced by firms is the mastery of the essential principles underlying effective risk management (Ali et al., 2018).

The concept of risk management encompasses a variety of methodologies and procedures employed to identify, quantify, monitor, and mitigate potential risks that may arise during the course of business operations conducted by a financial institution (Maldonado-Guzman et al., 2018). The advantages linked to the adoption of risk management practices have been identified based on the results of the 2018 National Survey of Risk Management conducted by the National Survey of Risk Management Studies. The elements included in this analysis consist of improvements in staff performance, employee satisfaction, efficient utilisation of resources, effectiveness and efficiency in supply-chain management, customer satisfaction, and service quality.

Several studies have described risk identification, risk assessment, risk response, and risk monitoring as the main stages of the risk management process. To accomplish this process, the key players in any project should have the skill to identify, assess, and be able to manage risks and ensure that risk information is effectively disseminated (Ali & Taylor, 2014; Aven, 2016; Gajewska & Ropel, 2011). Other studies have also described that the risk management technique contains a series of steps, namely, risk identification, risk analysis and prioritisation, risk response and risk control, and risk monitoring (Hamzah et al., 2015; Liu & Low, 2009; Mahendra et al., 2013). Risk management is perceived as a means to look into risks in a systematic way. On top of that, risk management is observed to identify sources of risks and uncertainties, determine the impact, develop an appropriate response, and deliberately determine how each risk should be treated (Ehsan et al., 2010). It is also perceived to be a process that creates value for a project and improves project performance in terms of cost, time, and quality (Siang & Ali, 2012).

A body of risk management literature has extensively examined risk management in the private sector. Some of the studies were done on Malaysian publicly listed companies (Abdurrahman et al., 2020), construction industries (Adeleke et al., 2020; Kang et al., 2015; Mustapha & Adnan, 2015), Islamic banks (Adam et al., 2023; Ariffin & Kassim, 2014), and small and medium enterprises (Ariffin & Kassim, 2014). Besides that, there is also a study related to the risk management model involving government-linked companies (Daud & Yazid, 2009) and the influence of the risk management officer and board of directors towards risk management implementation (Yazid et al., 2011).

Another body of literature has examined risk management in the public sector. These studies include factors needed in risk management implementation (Ilias et al., 2023), risk management and accountability (Bakar et al., 2016), risk management for Malaysian public-private partnership projects (Ahmad et al., 2018), risk management and analysis for local government (Hatvani, 2015), assessment of risk management practices in the Malaysian public sector (Said et al., 2020), and the implementation of risk management practices (Mustapha & Abidin, 2017). As a result, there are now opportunities for future studies to focus more on internal control and risk management in the public sector, which includes all stakeholders in the organisation.

4. Procurement in Public Sector

The systematic process of acquiring goods and services, as well as the subsequent financial settlement, is known as procurement. The duty of addressing the issue at hand is jointly held by both the public and private sectors. The act of purchasing goods or services entails a series of sequential steps, beginning with the first stages of planning and preparation and progressing towards the subsequent tasks of product or service identification, requirements assessment, supplier selection, and contract administration. Public procurement refers to the formal process through which government agencies and public sector organisations obtain products and services from suppliers. The public procurement process is regulated by a set of legal statutes, rules, and policies that are specifically intended to uphold principles of openness, impartiality, and accountability. The primary goal of public procurement is to provide optimal value for money by promoting competition and guaranteeing the proper utilisation of public funds (World Bank Group, 2020).

Private procurement, on the other hand, refers to the procurement activities carried out by firms and other bodies operating within the private sector. Market dynamics and the specific needs and preferences of an organisation both influence the regulation of private procurement. In contrast to public procurement, private procurement is characterised by the absence of specific legal frameworks or norms. Public procurement refers to the formal process used by government entities to obtain goods, services, and construction projects. The government has the responsibility of ensuring the effective implementation of the procurement process, adopting appropriate measures to protect the public interest, and guaranteeing the provision of public services of superior quality.

In the context of Malaysia, the term "government procurement" refers to the acquisition of goods, services, or a combination of both, conducted by a duly authorised agency under the Treasury, utilising federal funds (either in their entirety or partially) to support the agency's operations, facilitate the provision of government services, or serve the public interest (MOF, 2023). Circular P.K.1 (MOF, 2023) provides a comprehensive definition of the term "procurement". It encompasses various methods such as direct purchase (for supply, services, or work), direct appointment (for work), direct appointment with a specified cost limit (for consultant services), requisition (for work), quotation (for supply, services, or work), prequalification open tender (for supply, services, or work), open tender (for supply, services, or work), and request for proposal (RFP) (which falls under the category of open tender for supply, services, or work). These factors may help reduce the probability of issues arising and enhance the efficiency of the government's procurement process. The government procurement procedure includes the provision of guidelines and approval restrictions, which are outlined in Financial Circular P.K.2 (MOF, 2023). Rustiarini et al. (2019) conducted a study on high-risk sectors for fraudulent activities, whereby they identified procurement as an activity that is closely linked to the risk of procurement-related fraud.

Extensive research has been conducted in the past to investigate the correlation between procurement risk and instances of corruption and fraud. Kamal and Tohom (2019) conducted a study in Indonesia and found that there were a total of 171 cases of procurement fraud, representing 25% of the 688 recorded fraud cases. The findings also indicated a noticeable increase in the frequency of procurement corruption incidents. Additional risks associated with procurement include the occurrence of bribery and corruption, inadequate communication within the code of conduct, deficient fraud control mechanisms, a high volume of complaints, operational inefficiency and ineffectiveness, limited availability of human resources, a lack of accountability and transparency, mismanagement leading to public concern, wasteful utilisation of public funds, insufficient enforcement measures, and bribery and corruption within the local government of Malaysia (Azmi & Ismail, 2022; Othman et al., 2010; Pawi et al., 2012). Hence, it is essential to address the issue of risk management in procurement within both the commercial and public domains.

Ahmeti and Vladi (2017) argue that the implementation of risk management in the public sector is crucial due to its significant social implications. One may argue that risk management has significant importance within the public sector, particularly with regard to the allocation and acquisition of financial resources. As a result, finding, assessing, responding to, communicating, and monitoring any hazards that public sector companies may encounter might go more quickly. Furthermore, it may be argued that workers play a crucial role in facilitating the widespread adoption of risk management practices within the public sector. The comprehension of the need for risk management may be constrained as a result of the limits pertaining to risk management and internal control within public sector organisations in Malaysia.

5. Enterprise Risk Management

The use of enterprise risk management (ERM) has brought about a fresh perspective on the functioning of organisations. The comprehensive strategic approach of ERM is largely recognised as superior to conventional risk management practices (Banham, 2004). ERM is an essential endeavour for management, as it encompasses the process of identifying and assessing diverse hazards that possess the capacity to affect the operations and overall worth of a company. A strategic methodology is used to successfully tackle risk management from a complete organisational perspective, with the objective of building a comprehensive and efficient risk management policy. This enables organisations to enhance their understanding of potential dangers confronting the entity and evaluate the company's capacity to efficiently mitigate these risks. It is anticipated that this occurrence will result in a substantial enhancement in the overall efficiency and effectiveness of a company's operational activities.

The primary goal of ERM is to optimise the value of shareholders (Jones & Mwakipsile, 2017; Malarvizhi et al., 2018). This objective can be accomplished by enhancing capital efficiency through the establishment of an impartial framework for allocating corporate resources, identifying areas of elevated risk and proposing risk-based improvements, and implementing a process that assures all stakeholders of the organisation's commitment to prudent risk management. Based on the findings of the 1992 Cadbury Report, it is said that the primary responsibility for formulating risk management policies lies with the board of directors. This obligation is aimed at facilitating the cultivation of a comprehensive understanding of significant risks inside their respective organisations. According to Togok et al. (2016), ERM is indeed an integral part of an organisation.

Kleffner et al. (2003), however, noted that there is a lack of implementation of ERM programmes inside organisations. Even though there are positive effects of ERM implementation on firm performance, it is not widely practiced among Malaysian firms due to no specific rule for mandatorily implementing ERM (Togok et al., 2016). There are many factors contributing to the challenges faced in implementing ERM effectively. One such factor is a limited comprehension of how to accurately assess the advantages and efficacy of ERM implementation. Additionally, organisations have issues accurately evaluating risks and establishing correlations within their own internal operations. Other studies have emphasised that the primary obstacle to successful ERM implementation is the workers' lack of knowledge and comprehension of the ERM concept (Ali et al., 2019; Mustapha & Adnan, 2015). These studies showed that workers are likely to be the primary individuals who encounter and engage with these hazards throughout their routine work activities. Hence, the involvement of senior management and the engagement of workers at all organisational levels are crucial for ensuring effective ERM implementation.

According to Soltanizadeh et al. (2014), successful ERM implementation is contingent upon individuals' comprehension of risk management, risk assessment and analysis, risk control, and monitoring. A crucial aspect of achieving successful ERM implementation is ensuring that workers have knowledge about and comprehension of the underlying idea (Mustapha & Adnan, 2015). Other factors that may drive the adoption of ERM include considerations related to corporate governance, compliance with laws and regulations, external pressures, specific features of the company and industry, Chief Risk Officer (CRO) appointment, possible advantages, and prevailing business trends (Hudin & Abdul Hamid, 2014; Mustapha & Mustapa, 2020). On the other hand, there are studies that have observed that effective leadership skills in a Chief Executive Officer, a robust internal audit function, and the active participation of the CRO, senior management, and employees may facilitate the expeditious implementation of risk management practices inside government agencies (Ludin et al., 2017; Setapa & Zakwan, 2019). Nevertheless, the majority of these studies were mostly carried out within the confines of the private sector, resulting in a significant dearth of research pertaining to exams inside the public sector.

6. ERM Framework

Risk is an inherent component of any business venture and has emerged as a significant worry for stakeholders. The notion of risk is often linked to the likelihood of unfavourable events or transactions taking place during a certain period, resulting in adverse consequences for the achievement of objectives. This idea pertains to the potentiality of encountering an adverse consequence due to a certain occurrence. All companies would encounter a variety of hazards while enhancing their internal strategies and grappling with external challenges. In order to effectively contend for resources and establish a worldwide market presence, organisations must possess a sustainable competitive edge and maintain an ongoing need for innovation (Oliva, 2016).

The rapid pace of innovation and dynamic shifts in the global business landscape have presented significant possibilities for the corporation. Therefore, it is essential to adequately and promptly report hazards. Companies safeguard and generate value for their stakeholders through the identification of potential risks and opportunities. The identification and assessment of risks faced by an organisation, as well as the establishment of an appropriate risk tolerance level, pose significant challenges for management. These challenges are crucial in order to enhance value creation and mitigate the potential negative impacts of complex risks (Albasu & Nyameh, 2017; Beasley et al., 2017).

According to Hatvani (2015), the word "risk" encompasses both positive and negative implications of uncertainty in relation to fulfilling an organisation's requirements. According to the Financial Services Authority, a corporation is exposed to eight distinct categories of risks, including credit risk, market risk, liquidity risk, operational risk, compliance risk, legal risk, reputation risk, and strategic risk. Risk is inherently interconnected with uncertainty. Uncertain factors are more likely to engender dangers. Hence, effective risk management is

crucial in order to achieve the desired outcomes. In order to ensure the achievement of an organisation's goals and objectives, it is essential for the organisation's
leadership to possess the necessary skills and capabilities to successfully manage
any associated risks (Pawi et al., 2012). This viewpoint posits that the incorporation of risk management as a procedural framework may contribute to the enhancement of an organisation's decision-making process, hence accentuating its
progress, especially within the realm of public sector operations.

The first publication of a risk management standard occurred with the introduction of the Australian/New Zealand Standard (AS/NZS 4360: 1995). The
standard encompasses a variety of academic subjects (Marling et al., 2019), and
has undergone revisions in both 1999 and 2004. The development served as the
foundation for the establishment of the International Standards Organisation
(ISO). The publication of recommendations for best practices in risk management, namely ISO 31000:2018 (formerly ISO 31000:2009), was undertaken by
the Institute of Risk Management (IRM), a prominent professional organisation
in the field of risk management. According to the guidelines, ERM is characterised as a synchronised endeavour that oversees and governs organisations in
relation to risk.

ERM encompasses the expansion of the procedural framework to accommodate a wide array of potential threats. Moreover, it entails the formulation
of a complete strategic initiative that is readily available to all pertinent stakeholders, including shareholders and potential investors, and is included in their
yearly financial statements. The concept contains a collection of eight interrelated components that are derived from the organisation's management practices
and seamlessly integrated into the broader management process. The framework
encompasses several key components, namely: (i) the internal environment,
(ii) the process of objective definition, (iii) event identification, (iv) risk evaluation, (v) risk response formulation, (vi) control activity implementation, (vii)
information and communication management, and (viii) system monitoring
(ACCA, 2020).

The first release of the risk management standard ISO 31000:2009 was produced by the International Organisation for Standardisation (ISO) in 2009. The
second edition, ISO 31000:2018 (E) in Figure 1, was released in February 2018
as a replacement for the preceding edition. The revised iteration places significant emphasis on the organisation's commitment to prioritising development
and protection as its major objectives. Risk management is positioned as a crucial element of governance and leadership as well as an integral aspect of all
activities conducted within the company, hence emphasising its significance.
The ISO 31000:2018 standard delineates risk management into three distinct

components, namely methodology, framework, and principles. The International Organisation for Standardisation (ISO) emphasises the need to incorporate fundamental concepts into an organisation's risk management framework throughout its development process.

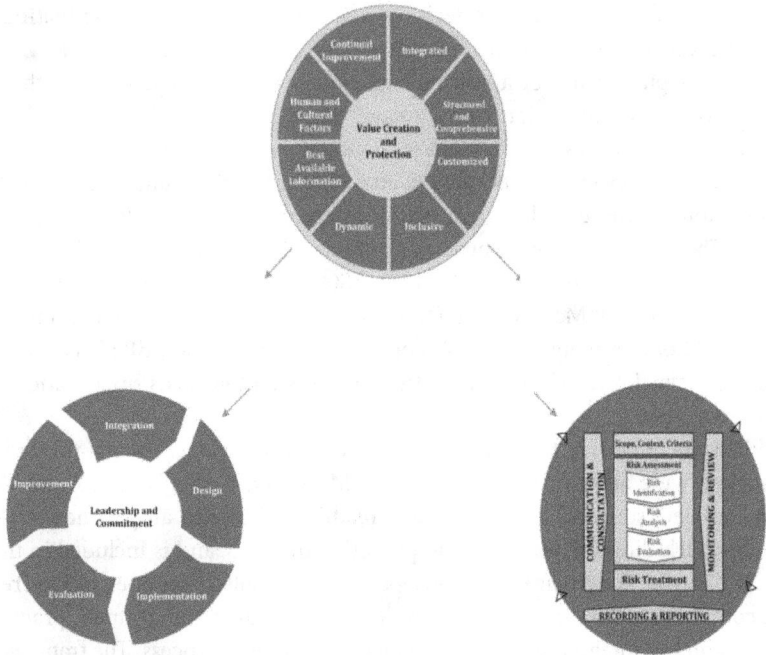

Figure 1. ISO Risk Management Framework
Adapted from ISO 31000:2018

Numerous businesses are also widely adopting the COSO ERM 2004 framework in addition to the ISO 31000:2009 standard. There are three distinct iterations of the COSO ERM framework, including the COSO ERM 2004 (Integrated Framework), COSO ERM 2014, and the revised COSO ERM 2017 (Integrating Strategy and Performance Framework) as in Figure 2. This study focused on analysing seven primary processes, namely objective setting, internal environment, information and communication, risk response, monitoring, risk assessment, and control activities, as outlined in the COSO ERM (2004). The aim was to enhance the comprehension of public employees regarding the initial model of risk management and internal control framework.

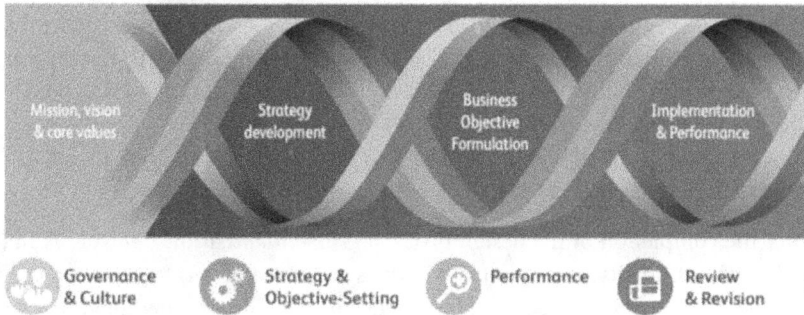

Figure 2. COSO Enterprise Risk Management Framework 2017
Adapted from COSO (2017)

The COSO ERM framework has undergone three successive changes, namely COSO ERM 2004 (Integrated Framework), COSO ERM 2014, and the most recent publication, COSO ERM 2017 (Integrating Strategy and Performance Framework). The methodology outlined by the Association of Certified Chartered Accountants (ACCA) (2022) encompasses a series of sequential processes:

1. The establishment of objectives by the board should be in accordance with the organisation's purpose and should be aligned with its risk tolerance. In order to effectively establish goals, it is essential for the board to possess a comprehensive understanding of the potential hazards that may arise from the pursuit of varied objectives.
2. The internal environment of a company establishes its tone, which affects its risk appetite, attitudes toward risk management, and ethical standards.
3. In order to facilitate the effective execution of managerial and staff responsibilities, it is essential for information systems to provide mechanisms that enable the identification, collection, and timely delivery of data. It is essential that the data provided to management is both relevant and of adequate quality. Furthermore, it is essential that it include all stated goals.
4. The selection of suitable management activities is crucial in aligning risks with risk tolerance and appetite. This stage is characterised by four basic responses: reduce, accept, transfer, and avoid.

5. It is important to consistently review and, if necessary, change the management system.
6. The process of assessing the probability and potential consequences of risks is used to determine the appropriate course of action in managing them. In order to effectively manage risks, it is essential for managers to not only assess the probability and consequences of individual risks but also consider their interdependencies.
7. It is important to adhere to established policies and processes in order to ensure the effectiveness of risk response measures.

After the completion of the design phase, it is essential that the controls exhibit optimal functionality, since control activities serve as a means to achieve a desired objective and are subject to the influence of individuals. Therefore, for prospective research endeavours, applying the COSO ERM (2017) together with the ISO 31000: 2018 framework is recommended to assess the level of risk management knowledge among public sector professionals.

6. ERM Framework in Malaysia

Since the occurrence of the 1997 financial crisis in Malaysia, a range of reforms have been implemented with the aim of ensuring transparency, accountability, and safeguarding the interests of shareholders. Consequently, the issuance of the Statement on Risk Management and Internal Control (Guideline for Directors of Listed Issuers), often referred to as RMIC 2013, took place in January 2013 by Bursa Malaysia. The Risk Management and Internal Control (RMIC) of 2013 replaced the previously released 2000 Statement on Internal Control, which provided guidance for directors of publicly listed firms. Participation in RMIC 2013 is of a voluntary nature. Nevertheless, this practice promotes the disclosure of hazards by organisations as well as the strategies used to mitigate these risks. The establishment of the RMIC in 2013 aimed to enhance governance practices together with the COSO ERM (2017) together with the ISO 31000: 2018 framework. Over time, there is an additional objective of enhancing openness among corporations, stakeholders, regulatory bodies, and the general public.

Additional standards and guidelines pertaining to the disclosure of risks for publicly listed companies in Malaysia encompass the following: (i) MFRS 7, which pertains to the disclosure of financial instruments; (ii) MFRS 9, which addresses financial instruments; (iii) MFRS 132, which focuses on the presentation of financial instruments; and (iv) Guidelines on Risk Management issued by Bank Negara Malaysia (BNM), which exclusively apply to financial institutions.

Two examples of the recommendations provided by Bank Negara Malaysia (BNM) are the "Risk Weighted Capital Adequacy Framework (RWCAF) – Disclosure Requirements (Pillar 3)" and the "Guidelines on Financial Reporting for Banking Institutions". The rules and accounting standards prioritise measurable risks, such as financial hazards, while neglecting other forms of risks, including operational risk and environmental risk (Ali & Taylor, 2014). In contrast to the optional nature of the instructions given by Bursa Malaysia, it should be noted that all the Malaysian Financial Reporting Standards (MFRSs) are obligatory. Failure to adhere to these criteria may result in substantial fines imposed by the respective regulatory authorities.

7. Conclusion

In conclusion, the ERM is an integral component of company strategy, including critical business operations and corporate culture (Fraser & Simkins, 2016). However, a review of the literature shows that the study of risk management in the public sector, particularly procurement, is still largely under-researched. The review also shows that the private sector often employs two prominent risk management frameworks, namely COSO ERM (2004) and ISO 31000 Risk Management. The use of these frameworks as appropriate advice for risk management and internal control practices is equally applicable in the public sector. This aligns with the findings of Irving and Walker (2021), who emphasised the need for implementing risk management practices inside the government sector. Kim (2014) argues that the implementation of risk management in the government sector has a dual purpose. It is not just aimed at controlling financial risk but also serves as a mechanism for managing crisis policy.

The public sector in Malaysia has gradually exhibited a gradual uptake of risk management and internal control implementation during its first stages, a phenomenon that is to be expected. Oulasvirta and Anttiroiko (2017) argue that the limited adoption of these procedures in local governments may be attributed to the prevalent practice of working in isolated and disconnected units. Moreover, the government lacks sufficient motivation to actively push the voluntary implementation of a complete risk management system. Of consequence, this creates a range of research opportunities to academics and researchers. Hence, this study proposes that the two frameworks provide a theoretical contribution to risk management within the public sector, with a specific focus on procurement. For example, the study potential for artificial intelligence (AI), machine learning, and big data analytics in enhancing risk assessment and mitigation within public procurement processes. Furthermore, an evaluation of the present competencies and aptitudes possessed by public procurement experts in the domain of risk management. Furthermore, there exists a potential for examining the effects of regulatory changes on risk profiles within the realm of public procurement.

References

Abdurrahman, A. P., Mohamad, S., Garrett, K. W. C., & Ehsanullah, S. (2020). Internal audit and enterprise risk management. *International Journal of Advanced Science and Technology, 29*(9), 401–409.

Adam, M., Soliman, A. M., & Mahtab, N. (2023). Measuring enterprise risk management implementation: A multifaceted approach for the banking sector. *The Quarterly Review of Economics and Finance, 87*(c.), 244–256.

ACCA. (2020). *COSO's enterprise risk management framework.* https://www. accaglobal.com/gb/en/student/exam-support-resources/professional-exams-study-resources/strategic-business-leader/technical-articles/coso-enterprise-risk-management-framework.html

Adeleke, A. Q., Nawi, M. N. M., & Abd-Karim, S. B. (2020). Where are we? The level of risk management in Malaysian construction industries. *International Journal of Supply Chain Management, 9*(1), 527–537.

Albasu, J., & Nyameh, J. (2017). Relevance of stakeholders theory, organizational identity theory and social exchange theory to corporate social responsibility and employees performance in the commercial banks in Nigeria. *International Journal of Business, Economics and Management, 4*(5), 95–105.

Ahmeti, R., &Vladi, B. (2017), Risk management in public sector: A literature review. *European Journal of Multidisciplinary Studies, 5*(1), 323–339.

Ali & Taylor, D. (2014a). Corporate risk disclosure in Malaysia: The influence of pre-dispositions of chief executive officers and chairs of audit committee. *Research Journal of Finance and Accounting, 5*(2), 92–106.

Ali, M. M., Ab Hamid, N. S., & Ghani, E. K. (2019). Examining the relationship between enterprise risk management and firm performance in Malaysia. *International Journal of Financial Research, 10*(3), 239–251.

Ali, Taylor, D., & Haron, N. H. (2018). Value relevance of risk disclosure by Malaysian public listed companies: The contributing effect of ownership structure. *Journal Herald National Academy of Managerial Staff of Culture and Arts, 1*(1), 920–926.

Aven, T. (2016). Risk assessment and risk management: Review of recent advances on their foundation. *European Journal of Operation Research, 253*(1), 1–13.

Ariffin, N. M., & Kassim, S. (2014). Risk management practices of selected Islamic banks in Malaysia. *Aceh International Journal of Social Science, 3*(1), 26–38.

Azmi, S. M. M., & Ismail, S. (2022, in press). Weaknesses of Malaysian public procurement: A review of auditor general's reports. *Journal of Financial Reporting and Accounting.*.

Beasley, M. S., Branson, B., & Hancock, B. (2017). The state of risk oversight: An overview of enterprise risk management processes. *European Journal of Operational Research, 253*(1), 1–13.

Banham, R. (2004). Enterprising views of risk management: Businesses can use ERM to manage a wide variety of risks. *Journal of Accountancy, 197*(6), 14–20.

Chakabva, O., Tengeh, R., & Dubihlela, J. (2021). Factors inhibiting effective risk management in emerging market SMEs. *Journal of Risk and Financial Management, 14*(6), 231.

Corvellec, H. (2009). The practice of risk management: Silence is not absence, *Risk Management, 11*, 285–304.

COSO. (2004). Enterprise risk management – integrated framework. https://www.coso.org/pages/erm.aspx

COSO. (2013a). COSO internal control – integrated framework. https://home.kpmg/content/dam/kpmg/pdf/2016/05/2750-New-COSO-2013-Framework-WHITEPAPER-V4.pdf

COSO. (2013b). *Transitioning to the 2013 COSO framework for external financial reporting purposes.* Ernst & Young LLP. https://nextstepac.com/wp-content/uploads/2018/10/1.6-EY-COSO-Transition-Questionnaire.pdf

COSO. (2004). *Enterprise risk management – integrated framework. The committee of sponsoring organizations of the tread-way commission.* https://www.coso.org/enterprise-risk-management

COSO. (2017). *Enterprise risk management: Integrating with strategy and performance.* https://www.coso.org/enterprise-risk-management

Daud, W. N. W., & Yazid, A. S. (2009). A conceptual framework for the adoption of enterprise risk management in government-linked companies. *International Review of Business Research Papers, 5*(5), 229–238.

Ehsan, N., Mirza, E., Alam, M., & Ishaque, A. (2010). Risk management in construction industry. Computer science and information technology (ICCSIT). *3rd IEEE International Conference*, pp. 16–21.

Fraser, J. R. S., & Simkins, B. J. (2016). The challenges of and solutions for implementing enterprise risk management. *Business Horizons, 59*(6), 689–698.

Gajewska, E., & Ropel, M. (2011). *Risk management practices in a construction project – a case study.* Publications Lib Chalmers Se, pp. 1–60. http://publications.lib.chalmers.se/records/fulltext/144253.pdf

Hamzah, A. R., Wang, C., & Farhanim, S. M. (2015). Implementation of risk management in the Malaysian construction industry: Case studies. *Journal of Construction Engineering*, 1–6.

Hatvani, E. N. C. (2015). Risk analysis and risk management in the public sector and in public auditing. *Public Finance Quarterly*, *1*(7), 7–28.

Hudin, N. S., & Abdul Hamid, A. B. (2014). Drivers to the implementation of risk management practices: A conceptual framework. *Journal of Advanced Management Science*, *2*(3), 163–171.

Ilias, A., Baidi, N., Ghani, E. K., & Omonov, A. (2023). A qualitative investigation on risk management implementation in the Malaysian public sector. *Economic Affairs*, *68*(2), 1247–1261.

Irving, J. H., & Walker, P. L. (2021). Applying enterprise risk management principles to the US government. *The CPA Journal*, *91*(4/5), 13.

ISO 31000:2009. *Risk management – principles and guidelines.* International Organisation for Standardisation (ISO).

ISO 31000:2018. *Risk management – principles and guidelines.* International Organisation for Standardisation (ISO).

Jones O. O., & Mwakipsile, G. (2017). Working capital management and managerial performance in some selected manufacturing firms in Edo State Nigeria. *Journal of Accounting, Business and Finance Research*, *1*(1), 46–55.

Kang, B. G., Fazlie, M. A., Goh, B. H., Song, M. K., & Zhang, C. (2015). Current practice of risk management in the Malaysia construction industry – the process and tools/techniques. *International Journal of Structural and Civil Engineering Research*, *4*(4), 371–377.

Kim, E. S. (2014). How did enterprise risk management first appear in the Korean public sector? *Journal of Risk Research*, *17*(2), 263–279.

Kleffner, A., Lee, R., & McGannon, B. (2003). The effect of corporate governance on the use of enterprise risk management: Evidence from Canada. *Risk Management and Insurance Review*, *6*(1), 53–73.

Lalonde, C., & Boiral, O. (2012). Managing risks through ISO31000: A critical analysis. *Risk Management*, *14*, 272–399.

Liu, J. Y., & Low, S. P. (2009). Developing an organizational learning-based model for risk management in Chinese construction firms. *Disaster Prevention and Management*, *18*(2), 170–186.

Ludin, K. R. M., Mohamed, Z. M., & Saleh, N. M. (2017). The association between CEO characteristics, internal audit quality and risk management implementation in the public sector. *Risk Management*, *19*, 281–300.

Malarvizhi, C. A., Nahar, R., & Manzoor, S. R. (2018). The strategic performance of Bangladeshi private commercial banks on post implementation relationship marketing. *International Journal of Emerging Trends in Social Sciences*, 2(1), 28–33.

Maldonado-Guzman, G., Marin-Aguilar, J., & Garcia-Vidales, M. (2018). Innovation and performance in Latin-American small family firms. *Asian Economic and Financial Review*, 8(7), 1008–1020.

Mahendra, P. A., Pitroda, J. R., & Bhavsar, J. J. (2013). A study of risk management techniques for construction projects in developing countries. *International Journal of Innovative Technology and Exploring Engineering*, 5, 139–142.

Marling, G., Horberry, T., & Harris, J. (2019). Development and validation of plain English intepretations of seven elements of the risk management process. *Safety*, 5(4), 75–85.

Maroofi, F., Ardalan, A. G., & Tabarzadi, J. (2017). The effect of sales strategies in the financial performance of insurance companies. *International Journal of Asian Social Science*, 7(2), 150–160.

Mustapha, W. M. W., & Abidin, N. H. Z. (2017). Internal audit and risk management practices among public universities in Malaysia. *IPN Journal of Research and Practice in Public Sector Accounting and Management*, 1, 1–14.

Mustapha, M., & Mustapah, N. J. (2020). Risk management practices of transportation companies: Practitioners' perspective. *International Journal of Business Continuity and Risk Management*, 10(2–3), 146–159.

MOF. (2013). *Malaysia's government procurement regime*.

Mustapha, M., & Adnan, A. (2015). A case study of enterprise risk management implementation in Malaysian construction firms. *International Journal of Economics and Financial Issues*, 5, 70–76.

Oliva, F. L. (2016). A maturity model for enterprise risk management. *International Journal of Production Economics*, 173, 66–79.

Oulasvirta, L., & Anttiroiko, A. V. (2017). Adoption of comprehensive risk management in local government. *Local Government Studies*, 43(3), 451–474.

Othman, R., Zakaria, H., Nordin, N., Shahidan, Z., & Jusoff, K. (2010). The Malaysian public procurements prevalent system and its weaknesses. *American Journal of Economics and Business Administration*, 2(1), 6–11.

Pawi, S., Juanil, D. M., Wan Yusoff, W. Z., & Shafie, F. (2012). Property tax performance of local authorities in Malaysia. *Proceeding Paper on International Conference on Management and Artificial Intelligence – ICMAI 2012*, Bali, Indonesia.

Reserve Bank of Australia. (2023). *The global financial crisis.* https://www. rba.gov.au/education/resources/explainers/pdf/the-global-financial-crisis. pdf?v=2023-10-04-16-56-42

Rustiarini, N., Sutrisno, S., Nurkholis, N., & Andayani, W. (2019). Fraud triangle in public procurement: Evidence from Indonesia. *Journal Of Financial Crime, 26*(4), 951–968.

Said, J., Alam, M. M., & Johari, R. J. (2020). Assessment of risk management practices in the public sector of Malaysia. *International Journal of Business and Emerging Markets, 12*(4), 377–390.

Setapa, M., & Zakwan, N. M. (2019). Enterprise risk management in Malaysian private higher educational institution. *Journal of Contemporary Social Science Research, 3*(1), 1–13.

Siang, L. C., & Ali, A. S. (2012). Implementation of risk management in the Malaysian construction industry. *Journal of Construction Engineering, 3*(1), 1–15.

Soltanizadeh, S., Rasid, S. Z. A., Golshan, N., Quoquab, F., & Basiruddin, R. (2014). Enterprise risk management practices among Malaysian firms. *Procedia – Social and Behavioral Sciences, 164*, 332–337.

Togok, S. H., Isa, C. R., & Zainuddin, S. (2016). Enterprise risk management adoption in Malaysia: A disclosure approach. *Asian Journal of Business and Accounting, 9*(1), 83–104.

World Bank Group. (2020). *Procurement in investment project financing: Goods, works, non-consulting and consulting services.* https://thedocs.worldbank.org/ en/doc/178331533065871195-0290022020/original/ProcurementRegulati ons.pdf

Yazid, A. S., Hussin, M. R., & Wan Daud, W. H. (2011), An examination of erm practices among the government-linked companies in Malaysia. *International Business Research, 4*(4), 94–105.

Nur Arini Mohamad Rusop, Nor Farizal Mohammed, & Nor
Aqilah Sutainim

Ethical Perception of Students on Earnings Management

1. Introduction

Due to the possibility of misleading information, earnings management can be considered as one of the many unethical practices. Prior studies have shown that earnings management is highly related to the firm's risk. Owing to the researchers' considerable concern on this matter, many of them conducted a study to investigate the students' perceptions of the ethical acceptability of these practices. This is because the students are the future accountants. The awareness in the educational stage is critical to reduce the risk of earnings management practices. Thus, this paper seeks to review the literature on the students' ethical perceptions of earnings management.

Earnings management is not a new phenomenon. Nevertheless, it has never posed such a threat to global financial system stability as it does now. According to Cygańska et al. (2019), the possibility of earnings management can be minimised by raising the ethical consciousness. Ethical education should be strengthened in its efficiency and effectiveness and its curricula should be better designed to allow young people to escape potential ethical traps in the future. Ethical attitudes are a significant variable in the decision-making process, especially when the decisions have social implications. Thus, accounting should also concentrate not only on accounting expertise and knowledge but also on the attitudes and behaviour of the individuals involved in the accounting processes. Furthermore, the accounting profession needs ethical practitioners with a high degree of ethical knowledge and sensitivity, capable of considering various variables in decision-making (Kutluk, 2017).

The early study conducted by Bruns and Merchant (1990) on the ethical acceptability by the students and accounting practitioners on earnings management practices, the result is labelled by the author as "frightening". They found that when a practice is not universally prohibited or a slight deviation from the related law and regulations, it tends to be accepted as an ethical practice by them regardless of who might suffer from those practices. There is a wide range of similar abroad studies have adopted and adapted the survey developed by Bruns and Merchant (1990), where either it was modified to suit the current situation, or it was taken and used as what it originally was (Cygańska et al., 2019; Sari et al., 2019). Numerous studies have selected business and accounting students as their participants as they are the potential future accountants in both private and public sectors (Cygańska et al., 2019; Kesaulya et al., 2019).

By and large, based on the past literature, the findings are still diverse and there is no unanimous answer on the ethical acceptability of earnings management practices yet. The study of ethical perceptions on earnings management is still relevant at the present time as the recent studies are considered as evidence that earnings management is still an ongoing phenomenon. Again, it is significant to use accounting students as the subject for this study since they are the ones who will be responsible for the company's account in the future. This study provides a review of literature discussing the ethical perceptions on earnings management in the perspective of accounting students.

2. Determinants of Ethical Perception

The following sections discuss the prior studies that examine factors that are associated with ethical perception. Among those possible factors are exam performance, family background, religiosity, and gender.

2.1. Exam Performance

Examination, or exam, is an important part of the educational system and has certain aims and objectives. According to Rasul and Bukhsh (2011), the examination evaluates the student's skill or accomplishments in any academic field. In every educational system, regardless of country and origin, the examinations are assessed for the students by giving them grades and positions based on their qualities and abilities. In other words, the examination is useful for educators to measure students' performance in their progress toward the predetermined goals. The accomplishment of particular goals in the activities centred around the educational environment is considered the academic outcome and achievement or performance, particularly in schools, colleges and universities (Kuanysh, 2017). From this, we can infer that the terms "academic achievement" and "academic performance" are equivalent to "exam performance" since both definitions refer to the outcomes from the educational environment.

According to Stiglbauer et al. (2013), since school-age children and adolescents usually spend most of their time in school, many academic factors broadly affect their subjective well-being. This may be due to the increasingly competitive school environment, which creates growing pressure for students to achieve academic success. Academic success also plays a role in diminishing problem behaviours (Zhang & Slesnick, 2020). This supports the finding of Maguin and Loeber (1996), which indicated that the educational achievement of adolescents is seen as an effective buffer for delinquency involvement. These researchers indicate that higher levels of academic performance foster behavioural outcomes among young people. This is further supported by Savage et al. (2017) whose study found that academic achievement has a strong relationship with individual physically aggressive or violent behaviours. This remarks that academic failure worsens behavioural problems due to conflict or estrangement from prosocial schoolmates and engaging with deviant peers.

However, there were also reports on which disagreed with the abovementioned arguments. For example, Seo (1995) found that high academic performance is not strongly associated with a lower level of problem behaviour among Asian Pacific Islanders. Besides, findings from Ismail and Rasheed (2019) which utilised the academic performance as one of the control variables also indicated that academic performance have no influence on future accountants' ethical judgments in Malaysia. From this, it is clear that most of studies have found the similar result, on which, there is a negative correlation between academic performance and problematic or unethical behaviour.

A great number of studies investigated the effect of certain factors towards the exam performance of students. These include the effect of school size, online quizzes and slides, class attendance, exam anxiety and others. However, the impact of academic performance on youth behavioural outcomes are less known (Zhang & Slesnick, 2020). Accordingly, only a limited amount of literature that discusses the effect of exam performance on an individual's certain behaviours or attitudes can be found. Therefore, investigating whether the exam performance of accounting students could influence their perceptions on the ethicality of earnings management scenarios can fill in this research gap.

2.2. Family Background

Hofstede (2001) has proposed that the way people around the world think, feel and act with the issues they experience and their decisions are primarily influenced by their social environments. The social environment comprises many dimensions and family is one of it. Family is the term widely used by the majority of people in order to describe a group of people that are related either by recognised birth or marriage relationship. According to Collins et al. (2012), ideally, as family members grow and engage in the community, the families will provide predictability, structure and protection. It is the family that establishes the foundations for the children's moral and spiritual development, and also concerns the concept of right and wrong as well as good and bad.

According to Arulmoly and Kiruthika (2017), the term "family background" can be defined as all the objects, forces and, circumstances and conditions in the home which give impact to the child physically, intellectually and emotionally. The background of the family can be seen in terms of multiple aspects. This encompasses the highest educational level, professional qualifications, reputation, occupation, position, social status and other relevant facts about the family members. In this study, family background is measured by assessing the monthly income as family income is the most critical predictor of educational attainment, holding all other factors constant (Padilla, 1996).

Adequate family income would help their children's development since parents can adequately provide primary and secondary needs of children (Khanifah et al., 2019). It is also suggested that the higher an individual's economic status, the more consumptively he appears to behave which means an individual's socio-economic status (SES) also related to his ethical behaviour. In the same way, a prior research also identified a positive association between parental SES and children's cognitive ability (Damian et al., 2015). The authors further explained that this may be due to the parents with lower SES who provide lesser positive experiences for their kids, as the family stress model proposed. Likewise, higher SES parent provides more cognitively stimulating experiences for their children, as the family investment model contended. Consequently, both factors are thought to affect children's cognitive ability development.

However, there is an indication that someone with a high SES may also behave unethically because their social status makes them think about their own interests (Khanifah et al., 2019). Kurniawan and Anjarwati (2020) found that family SES has a significant negative relationship with ethical perceptions of accounting students. This can be due to selfishness, dishonesty and consumptivity.

Other than that, several other literatures highlighted the importance of family background in influencing their family members' educational attainment (Sewell & Hauser, 1975) and moral reasoning (Arsenio & Gold, 2006). From this, we could see the indirect relationship between the family background and ethical perception on earnings management. Although several past studies investigated the effect of family background on children's outcomes (educational attainment, dropping out behaviour, delinquency, etc.), there is a lack of prior literature investigating the association of family background and ethical perception on earnings management practices. Hence, it is necessary to explore further the influence of accounting students' family background on their perceptions of the ethicality of earnings management scenarios.

2.3. Religiosity

Issues related to religion and spirituality's role in business and accounting ethics have received increasing attention in recent years. Religiosity, as defined by Bloodgood et al. (2008), is a process of understanding, committing to, and following a set of religious doctrines or principles. Nazaruddin et al. (2018) defined it as an integrated system of institutions, lifestyles, beliefs, and ritual activities that provides meaning to human life and guides them to the highest or sacred values. An individual's religiosity can be measured by using several indicators such as the frequency of their attendance at religious services, religious affiliation, prayer frequency, reading of sacred texts, and participation in religious discussions with others (Bloodgood et al., 2008).

The religiosity of students is closely related to ethical perceptions on earnings management practices, which is the main concern of this study since it could impact their moral and ethical reasoning in judging such practices. Besides, Sari et al. (2019) stated that individuals' beliefs reflect their behaviour. The beliefs of individuals motivate them to behave ethically or unethically in achieving their objectives. This is supported by Ismail and Rasheed (2019) who posited that to some extent, the likelihood that individuals will behave ethically or unethically depends on the personal values motivating them to assess their actions. According to (Clark & Dawson, 1996), a person's religiousness is a possible source of ethical norms and therefore, it impacts ethical reasoning. Besides, fairness and integrity are central to religious teachings. Faithful adherents of religion are often believed to be far from a moral act because religious teachings direct people to be honest (Hadjar, 2017).

According to Cai et al. (2020), religions prohibit unethical decisions, including earnings management, by offering moral guidance and defining managerial principles. Religion is one of the mechanisms that helps a person to avoid unethical behaviour, especially in business operations (Nazaruddin et al., 2018). In addition, religion is perhaps the foundation of ethics in society and offers an implicit rationale for many moral acts such as safe working conditions, equal treatment of employees and environmental protection (Keller et al., 2007). Besides, prior researchers have also found that religious education and beliefs can influence an individual's behaviour by offering a context and framework to help them distinguish between right and wrong (Magill, 1992). Anyone with a high degree of religiosity should be able to regulate themselves to carry out ethical acts, to do good and not hurt others in compliance with their religious teachings.

However, in contrast with the numerous studies reporting that the highly religious individuals will have higher ethical sensitivity, several studies have also discovered distinct results. Besides, a study conducted by Sari et al. (2019) indicated that religious-based university students consider earnings management to be more ethically acceptable than those in public university students. These phenomena supported the Sacred Canopy Theory which argues that high materialism caused religious values to fade. Furthermore, Kurniawan and Anjarwati (2020), which investigated the influence of religiosity on accounting students' ethical perception, found a negative relationship among those variables. The results indicated that when the students' level of religiosity is high, their ethical perceptions are low. The authors further explained that people practising religion will not necessarily behave ethically. This is due to pressure factors that cause them to act unethically. From the above review, it is found that religiosity is an essential factor on one person's behaviour. The mixed results prompt above further investigation on the relationship between religiosity and ethical perception on earnings management.

2.4. Gender

According to Lucyanda and Endro (2014) and Diamond (2020), gender is a term that refers to social or cultural distinctions associated with being male or female. Gender identity is the degree to which one identifies as being either masculine or feminine. In cognitive psychology and management literature, it has been long recognised that the conservatism, risk aversion, and ethical behaviour are significantly different according to gender (Bernardi & Arnold, 1997). This is supported by Gilligan's (1993) study which suggests that there is a variation in morality between men and women from the early socialisation process. Women tend to be socialised to display compassion and caring, while men often are more competitive and more concerned with justice (Devonish et al., 2009). In terms of decision-making, women are typically expected to consider friendships, obligations and empathy for others which results in ethical dilemmas. On the other hand, men tend to focus on rules, rights, fairness, and justice in resolving ethical problems (Peterson et al., 2001).

Landry et al. (2004) deduced that gender has influenced on the development of the concept of selfishness, justice, deontology, relativism and utilitarianism. In addition, while not directly related to earnings management, prior research (Eaton & Giacomino, 2001) suggests that women's moral development is higher than that of their male counterparts. Furthermore, Khanifah et al. (2019) also hold that when identifying and understanding the ethical and unethical, women are more ethically sensitive as compared to men, and women have a stronger moral context and development than men. In addition, women are more likely to serve their authority while men who are more aggressive and bigger have more recognition of achievement than those women. According to Birnberg (2011), given the fact that gender issues continue to draw increasing interest in behavioural accounting research, the impact of gender on accounting decisions has not been thoroughly explored and needs further analysis.

In the realm of accounting, Heminway (2007) claimed that females tend to be more truthful than males and thus, are less likely to exploit corporate information. Peni and Vähämaa (2010) found that female Chief Financial Officers (CFOs) involve in less earnings management activities as compared to male CFOs. According to Deshpande (1997), which studied business managers, found that the ethical viewpoints vary according to gender. Furthermore, Betz et al. (2013) explored sex gaps between students at business school, concentrating on work-related beliefs and willingness to engage in unethical behaviour. They found that men were more than twice as likely to engage in unethical behaviour. A study conducted by McCabe et al. (2006) concluded that men are more willing than women to behave unethically and women are significantly more likely than men to view certain questionable acts as unethical. On the other hand, there is also a study that found males are more ethical than females (Bossuyt & Van Kenhove, 2018).

Despite numerous studies reporting gender differences in ethical attitudes, a number of other studies did not identify any major gender-related differences. Clikeman et al. (2001) examined students' perceptions on earnings management practices and concluded that gender shows no significant differences. Even after controlling the impact of nationality, the results remain similar. Besides, Odar et al. (2017) discovered that there is no statistically significant difference between male and female professionals in regard to the most earnings management scenarios. Hermawan and Kokthunarina (2018) provided the evidence that gender has no significant relationship with the ethical perception of accounting students in Indonesia. Chandra et al. (2016) which investigated the gender as another variable that are predicted to influence the ethical behaviours of the students in the task relating to due diligence found that gender did not significantly influence the ethical behaviours of students. Therefore, further research is needed to gain comprehensive understanding of how gender affects ethical decision-making, particularly in the field of accounting and earnings management.

3. Conclusion

This paper reviews the literature related to ethical perception of accounting students on earnings management. Earnings management is important as it affects the information reported in the financial statements. If a decision is made using inaccurate information, the decision is doubtful and can create several issues for both the business and the users of the financial statements (Hamid et al., 2016). Thus, the awareness on earnings management from the higher education is critical. Besides, with good ethics education, they are expected to benefit the profession in the long run. The study highlights vital factors that may affect accounting students' ethical perception on earnings management practices. The examination of these factors is essential as the students are the ones who will serve the company as an accountant and who will directly manage the company's accounts in the future.

Acknowledgement

The authors would like to extend their gratitude to the Accounting Research Institute, HiCOE and Universiti Teknologi MARA for funding this research under the Bestari Grant – Islamic Financial Criminology, with reference number 600-RMC/DANA 5/3/BESTARI (TD) (010/2022)

References

Arsenio, W. F., & Gold, J. (2006). The effects of social injustice and inequality on children's moral judgments and behavior: Towards a theoretical model. *Cognitive Development*, *21*(4), 388–400. https://doi.org/10.1016/j.cogdev.2006.06.005

Arulmoly, C., & Kiruthika, A. (2017). the Impact of parental involvement on students' attitude and performance in science in senior secondary grades in Batticaloa educational zone. *Sri Lanka. Asian Journal of Multidimensional Research*, *6*(5), 66.

Bernardi, R. A., & Arnold, D. F. (1997). An examination of moral development within public accounting by gender, staff level, and firm. *Contemporary Accounting Research*, *14*(4), 653–668. https://doi.org/10.1111/j.1911-3846.1997.tb00545.x

Betz, M., O'Connell, L., & Shepard, J. M. (2013). Gender differences in proclivity for unethical behavior. Citation Classics from *The Journal of Business Ethics: Celebrating the First Thirty Years of Publication*, 427–432. https://doi.org/10.1007/978-94-007-4126-3_20

Birnberg, J. (2011). A proposed framework for behavioral accounting research. *Behavioral Research in Accounting, 23*(1), 1–43.

Bloodgood, J. M., Turnley, W. H., & Mudrack, P. (2008). The influence of ethics instruction, religiosity, and intelligence on cheating behavior. *Journal of Business Ethics, 82*(3), 557–571. https://doi.org/10.1007/s10551-007-9576-0

Bossuyt, S., & Van Kenhove, P. (2018). Assertiveness bias in gender ethics research: Why women deserve the benefit of the doubt: Marketing and consumer behavior. *Journal of Business Ethics, 150*(3), 727–739. https://doi.org/10.1007/s10551-016-3026-9

Bruns, W. J., & Merchant, K. A. (1990). The dangerous morality of managing earnings. *Management Accounting, 72*(2), 22.

Burnett, A. J., Enyeart Smith, T. M., & Wessel, M. T. (2016). Use of the social cognitive theory to frame university students' perceptions of cheating. *Journal of Academic Ethics, 14*(1), 49–69. https://doi.org/10.1007/s10805-015-9252-4

Cai, G., Li, W., & Tang, Z. (2020). Religion and the method of earnings management: Evidence from China. *Journal of Business Ethics, 161*(1), 71–90. https://doi.org/10.1007/s10551-018-3971-6

Chandra, A., Calderon, T. G., & Welfley, M. M. (2016). Reporting truthfully: Assessing ethical behavior of accounting students. *Journal of Forensic & Investigative Accounting, 8*(1).

Clark, J. W., & Dawson, L. E. (1996). Personal religiousness and ethical judgements: An empirical analysis. *Journal of Business Ethics, 15*(3), 359–372. https://doi.org/10.1007/BF00382959

Clikeman, P. M., Geiger, M. A., & O'Connell, B. T. (2001). Student perceptions of earnings management: The effects of national origin and gender. *Teaching Business Ethics, 5*(4), 389–410.

Collins, D., Jordan, C., & Coleman, H. (2012). *Brooks/Cole empowerment series: An introduction to family social work.* Nelson Education.

Cygańska, M., Artienwicz, N., & Burchart, R. (2019). The ethical judgments of Polish accounting students regarding earnings management. *Theoretical Journal of Accounting, 104*(160), 21–36. https://doi.org/10.5604/01.3001.0013.4354

Damian, R. I., Su, R., Shanahan, M., Trautwein, U., & Roberts, B. W. (2015). Can personality traits and intelligence compensate for background disadvantage? Predicting status attainment in adulthood. *Journal of Personality and Social Psychology, 109*(3), 473–489. https://doi.org/10.1037/pspp0000024

Deshpande, S. P. (1997). Managers' perception of proper ethical conduct: The effect of sex, age, and level of education. *Journal of Business Ethics, 16*(1), 79–85. https://doi.org/10.1023/A:1017917420433

Devonish, D., Alleyne, P. A., Cadogan-McClean, C., & Greenidge, D. (2009). An empirical study of future professionals' intentions to engage in unethical business practices. *Journal of Academic Ethics, 7*(3), 159–173. https://doi.org/10.1007/s10805-009-9096-x

Diamond, M. (2020). Sex and gender are different: Sexual identity and gender identity are different. *Clinical Child Psychology & Psychiatry, 7*(3), 320–334.

Eaton, T., & Giacomino, D. (2001). An examination of personal values: Differences between accounting students and managers and differences between genders. *Teaching Business Ethics, 5*(2), 213–229. https://doi.org/10.1023/A:1011444127775

Gilligan, C. (1993). *In a different voice: Psychological theory and women's development.* Harvard University Press.

Hadjar, I. (2017). The effect of religiosity and perception on academic cheating among Muslim students in Indonesia. *Journal of Education and Human Development, 6*(1). https://doi.org/10.15640/jehd.v6n2a15

Hamid, F., Hashim, H. A., & Salleh, Z. (2016). Auditors' view on acceptability of clients' earnings management practices. *Corporate Ownership & Control, 13*(4), 535–541.

Heminway, J. M. (2007). Sex, trust, and corporate boards. *Hastings Women's Law Journal, 18*(173). https://doi.org/10.2139/ssrn.924590

Hermawan, M. S., & Kokthunarina. (2018). Factors influencing accounting students' perception of accounting ethics: An empirical study in Indonesia. *Jurnal Akuntansi Dan Bisnis, 18*(2), 88–97.

Hofstede, G. (2016). Culture's consequences: Comparing values, behaviors, institutions, and organizations across nations. *Collegiate Aviation Review, 34*(2), 108.

Ismail, S., & Rasheed, Z. (2019). Influence of ethical ideology and emotional intelligence on the ethical judgement of future accountants in Malaysia. *Meditari Accountancy Research, 27*(6), 805–822. https://doi.org/10.1108/MEDAR-04-2018-0326

Keller, A. C., Smith, K. T., & Smith, L. M. (2007). Do gender, educational level, religiosity, and work experience affect the ethical decision-making of U.S. accountants? *Critical Perspectives on Accounting, 18*(3), 299–314. https://doi.org/10.1016/j.cpa.2006.01.006

Kesaulya, F. A., Putri, W., & Khairunnisa. (2019). Does ethical context affect the ethicality related judgement by the observers of earnings management? *Journal of Accounting and Strategic Finance, 2*(2), 107–116.

Khanifah, K., Isgiyarta, J., Lestari, I., & Udin, U. (2019). The effect of gender, locus of control, love of money, and economic status on students' ethical perception. *International Journal of Higher Education*, 8(5), 168–175. https://doi.org/10.5430/ijhe.v8n5p168

Kuanysh, A. Z. (2017). The effect of single-sex school on students' academic achievements. *International Scientific and Practical Conference World Science*, 4(9), 34–44.

Kurniawan, A., & Anjarwati, A. (2020, March). Does love of money, Machiavellian, religiosity, socioeconomic status, and understanding of the accountant's code of ethics affect the ethical perception of accounting students? In *1st international conference on accounting, management and entrepreneurship (ICA-MER 2019)* (pp. 33–37). Atlantis Press. https://doi.org/10.2991/aebmr.k.200305.009

Kutluk, F. A. (2017). Behavioral accounting and its interactions. *Accounting and Corporate Reporting – Today and Tomorrow*. https://doi.org/10.5772/intechopen.68972

Landry, R., Moyes, G. D., & Cortes, A. C. (2004). Ethical perceptions among Hispanic students: Differences by major and gender. *Journal of Education for Business*, 80(2), 102–108. https://doi.org/10.3200/joeb.80.2.102-108

Lucyanda, J., & Endro, G. (2014). Faktor-faktor yang Mempengaruhi Perilaku Etis Mahasiswa Akuntansi Universitas Jember. *Jurnal Ekonomi Dan Ilmu Sosial Universitas Bakrie*.

Magill, G. (1992). Theology in business ethics: Appealing to the religious imagination. *Journal of Business Ethics*, 11(2), 129–135. https://doi.org/10.1007/BF00872320

Maguin, E., & Loeber, R. (1996). Academic performance and delinquency. *Crime and Justice*, 20, 145–264. https://doi.org/10.1086/449243

McCabe, A. C., Ingram, R., & Dato-On, M. C. (2006). The business of ethics and gender. *Journal of Business Ethics*, 64(2), 101–116. https://doi.org/10.1007/s10551-005-3327

Nazaruddin, I., Rezki, S. B., & Rahmanda, Y. (2018). Love of money, gender, religiosity: The impact on ethical perceptions of future professional accountants. *Business and Economic Horizons*, 14(2), 424–436. https://doi.org/10.15208/beh.2018.31

Odar, M., Jerman, M., Jamnik, A., & Kavčič, S. (2017). Accountants' ethical perceptions from several perspectives: Evidence from Slovenia. *Economic Research-Ekonomska Istrazivanja*, 30(1), 1785–1803. https://doi.org/10.1080/1331677X.2017.1392885

Padilla, Y. C. (1996). The influence of family background on the educational attainment of Latinos. *New England Journal of Public Policy*, 11(2), 5. http://scholarworks.umb.edu/nejpp/vol11/iss2/5

Peni, E., & Vähämaa, S. (2010). Female executives and earnings management. *Managerial Finance*, *36*(7), 629–645. https://doi.org/10.1108/0307435101 1050343

Peterson, D., Rhoads, A., & Vaught, B. C. (2001). Ethical beliefs of business professionals: A study of gender, age and external factors. *Journal of Business Ethics*, *31*(3), 225–232. https://doi.org/10.1023/A:1010744927551

Rasul, S., & Bukhsh, Q. (2011). A study of factors affecting students' performance in examination at university level. *Procedia – Social and Behavioral Sciences*, *15*, 2042–2047. https://doi.org/10.1016/j.sbspro.2011.04.050

Sari, R. C., Sholihin, M., & Ratmono, D. (2019). Do ethics education and religious environment mitigat e creative accounting? In *Character education for 21st century global citizens* (pp. 307–312). Routledge.

Savage, J., Ferguson, C. J., & Flores, L. (2017). The effect of academic achievement on aggression and violent behavior: A meta-analysis. *Aggression and Violent Behavior*, *37*, 91–101. https://doi.org/10.1016/j.avb.2017.08.002

Seo, D. (1995). Some "A" students lead dual lives as gang-bangers: The Asian American says they are torn between values of parents, friends. Some engage in serious crime. *Los Angeles Times*, *1*. https://www.latimes.com/archives/la-xpm-1995-07-05-mn-20437-story.html

Sewell, W. H., & Hauser, R. M. (1975). *Education, occupation, and earnings*. Academic Press.

Stiglbauer, B., Gnambs, T., Gamsjäger, M., & Batinic, B. (2013). The upward spiral of adolescents' positive school experiences and happiness: Investigating reciprocal effects over time. *Journal of School Psychology*, *51*(2), 231–242. https://doi.org/10.1016/j.jsp.2012.12.002

Zhang, J., & Slesnick, N. (2020). Academic performance and delinquent and aggressive behaviors among children with substance using mothers. *Children and Youth Services Review*, *109*, 104683. https://doi.org/10.1016/j.childyo uth.2019.104683